0

Advance Praise for
Millennials' Guide to Workplace Politics

"Millennials' Guide to Workplace Politics distills the lessons and wisdom of countless research studies and individual experiences into grounded steps and questions for seeing an issue clearly. While reading this book, I found myself reflecting often on the (many) times that I have failed to apply these steps and ask these questions in my own professional journey. Drs. Mira Brancu and Jennifer Wisdom provide simple tools and suggestions that give new professionals a jump start on (and more seasoned professionals a reminder of) the realization that general ideas like "trust your feelings," "your work will speak for itself," and "just be yourself" are not likely to help you achieve your professional goals. I also appreciate the way this book empowers the reader to take control of their professional journey through self-awareness, problem evaluation, skill-building, and intentional action with reflection. This is an excellent guide in the continuing challenge to navigate the politics of the workplace while maintaining personal values and integrity."

    -**Bradley Brummel,** PhD, Associate Professor of Psychology, The University of Tulsa, Millennial-Adjacent

"Millennials' Guide to Workplace Politics really feels like a pocket-sized mentor, containing perspectives and advice that are sure to resonate with other professionals like me. As a Millennial who started her career working in a start-up, a non-profit, then a government job, I understand how overwhelming office politics can be, and this book finds such a good balance between providing productive and positive advice while not talking down to the reader or sugar-coating the challenges. Drs. Mira Brancu and Jennifer Wisdom offer such a useful and refreshing take on professional relationships; counter to the commonly held workplace belief that emotions should be checked at the door, they smartly make it clear that professional conduct can and should include emotional intelligence. Emphasizing the importance of creating safe and supportive professional environments is both

productive and consistent with the commonly held values of young professionals like myself! I also love that it includes specific advice for virtual workplaces, a new experience for many of us and one unlikely to go away anytime soon! And I love how it's formatted – it's perfect to use as a reference, and the many cross-references make it so easy to find more advice specific to a predicament or situation. If you are a Millennial professional (or any professional looking to navigate office politics), I highly recommend this book for its actionable advice, insightful analyses, and the tools it provides that can be readily implemented to support and advance your career."

    -**Meredith Burger,** Working Millennial

"Millennials' Guide to Workplace Politics is an incredible resource whether you are just getting started in your career or are looking to take it to the next level. Drs. Mira Brancu and Jennifer Wisdom offer a comprehensive overview of the wide range of politics you will encounter throughout your career and provide sage advice for how to navigate and thrive in complex, real-world situations. There is so much packed into here and it's going to be eye opening and helpful for a lot of people."

    -**Kate Scott,** MS, MBA, Organizational Development and Workplace Strategy Expert

"This savvy survival guide for climbing the company ladder is a fabulous read for anyone who wants to win with integrity and practicality. It's brilliantly laced with emotional and adaptability intelligence. Each chapter offers insight for where you are and where you wish to be if you're honest about who you are and what you can be. Anyone reading *Millennials' Guide to Workplace Politics* (especially young, ambitious women) will not just learn how to work the room but will learn how to develop professionally."

    -**Ariel Shivers-McGrew,** MA, LPC, Business Owner, PhD Student, Military Service Member, Millennial

"*Millennials' Guide to Workplace Politics* is incredibly actionable, and it's a guide meant to flip through and find solutions. I envision it being widely highlighted and ear marked. It is such a meaningful accomplishment that will help a lot of people! This is also a great guide for a coach helping Millennials navigate these workplace issues."

   -**Stefanie Mockler,** PhD, Leadership Coach & Founder of The Female Leader's Edge, Millennial

"This is an easy-to-read reference book that could serve many functions, including a library of development suggestions. I can see how it can be used as part of a coaching process, particularly after the assessment process. I can't wait to hand out copies to my millennial friends and colleagues and recommend to my coaching clients."

   -**Kristin Powell,** PhD, Organizational and Leadership Consultant, DE&I Expert

"*Millennials' Guide to Workplace Politics* is that in-between step I've been looking for regarding getting into consultation work and better understanding the politics embedded in the workplace. I particularly found the chapter on how to ask for useful feedback applicable because as someone who experiences impostor syndrome, workplace politics can make you wary of asking how to improve. The personal reflections that Drs. Brancu and Wisdom share throughout this book are witty, personable, and super helpful. Do yourself a favor, and grab this book!"

   -**Daniel Lattimore,** MS, NCC, Counseling Psychology Doctoral Candidate

MILLENNIALS'
GUIDE TO
WORKPLACE
POLITICS

What No One Ever Told You About
Power and Influence

WINDING PATHWAY BOOKS

Mira Brancu, PhD
Jennifer P. Wisdom, PhD MPH ABPP

Published by Winding Pathway Books

WINDING PATHWAY BOOKS

ISBN (print): 978-1-954374-91-1
ISBN (e-book): 978-1-954374-90-4
Cover design by Diego G. Diaz
Photo credit: Diego G. Diaz and Allie Mullin

For more information or bulk orders, visit: www.leadwithwisdom.com

Printed in the United States of America

TABLE OF CONTENTS

FOREWORD

Dear Reader,

As a Millennial working in the corporate sector, I made a mental choice not to engage in workplace politics. I decided that I would double-down on my strengths, develop my weaknesses, and grow in new ways. But as for engaging in office or workplace politics? That was a strong no for me.

Or so I thought.

When I decided that I was going to enter the marketing world as an Industrial-Organizational Psychologist, I knew it would be uncharted territory. Marketing isn't seen as an essential skill or ability to the competency development of an Industrial-Organizational Psychologist. In fact, many Industrial-Organizational Psychologists struggle with helping others to understand what they do. I always hear comments like, "I don't know how to explain Industrial-Organizational Psychology", "my family thinks I'm like Human Resources", or "Industrial-Organizational Psychology is too complex to break down". But if I was going to truly carve out a niche for myself and be able to coach Industrial-Organizational Psychologists on how to brand and market their services, I needed to learn from the best. So, I used LinkedIn to connect with the president of a prominent marketing firm and bartered for a 6-month engagement with me coaching junior executives and him coaching me on all things marketing consulting. As a result of this successful set-up, I was hired into a full-time position.

As I became immersed in the culture of the company, I had my original goals in mind: (1) double-down on my strengths, (2) develop my weaknesses, and (3) grow in new ways. But after being thrown under the bus for something that had nothing to do with me, I realized I couldn't escape workplace politics. It was apparent that I lacked the awareness and skills I needed to deal with team members who didn't operate with the same principles I did.

So, when I was invited to review this new book on workplace politics, I knew it was time to get equipped and empowered to approach this topic head on.

What you are now holding in your hands not only educated me on workplace politics, but also has added a critical component to my personal and professional development. For too long, leadership and self-help books have led me to believe it's as simple as using a model, following the latest thought leaders, or getting a coach. This is not another one of those self-help books. This is a survival manual and tactical strategy plan to properly engage with workplace politics in such a way that you grow and develop as an early career leader.

The authors present clearly defined workplace politics: the good, the bad, and the questionable. They also present a solid case for why you should engage in workplace politics and practical ways to navigate this arena. This book has empowered and equipped me to handle workplace politics that are inevitable and work with my team and my leaders for lasting change within the organization and within myself.

Dr. NaTasha Jordan, PhD
Director of Consulting - The Sasha Group

INTRODUCTION

When we say the word "politics", some of us bristle, conjuring up images of the "dirty politics" used in backroom self-serving decision-making. When we say, "I'm not going to play games and involve myself in politics," what we really mean is "I'm sick and tired of unprincipled and amoral politics and I refuse to engage in that kind of abuse of power." The term politics has become mostly overtaken by negative, sometimes abusive, political tactics that are associated with selfish pursuits of personal power. Many of us want to push "politics" as far away from us as possible.

We define workplace politics as *the processes and behaviors between people in a workplace that include power, authority, communication, and networking to create change that benefits the organization or people within it.* Workplace politics, moreover, are part of everyday life. Talented managers and leaders who do not engage in work politics often get left out of the important decision-making process and fail to progress or thrive in their career. Politics come in many forms, with the self-serving, cutthroat type being only one – and that is an unhealthy type! There are also positive, "honest" politics that can help you become a better leader when used appropriately. All politics can be intentional or unintentional. This book will help you take a more intentional approach.

We have worked in organizations collectively for more than 40 years. We have seen elegant and powerful positive use of politics:

- Managers obtaining funds to move forward projects that had been stagnant for years.
- Directors carving out time for staff to have professional development training and improve their performance.
- Leaders listening to customers and staff to implement processes to increase transparency, responsiveness, and customer satisfaction.
- Bosses helping staff and managers navigate transitions in a healthy way and ensure ongoing positive relationships.

3

- Leaders choosing to sponsor, mentor, and support earlier career individuals who demonstrate high potential.
- Senior executive leaders who provide managers and directors opportunities to lead challenging projects and gain positive visibility in the company.

We have also seen self-serving and cutthroat politics damage staff, the organization, and even customers:

- A manager who tried to take over my (JPW) space and use my staff for her projects. I learned it was definitely important to practice defensive politics!
- A manager who did not stop a dysfunctional team from undermining and gossiping, held back progress until he was sure he got credit, and operated a fiefdom with a very narrow range of acceptable behavior.
- A leader who actively cultivated a persona across the company as kind, caring, and respectful, but who also regularly yelled and cursed at staff, leading several to leave due to stress reactions.
- Directors who systematically and repeatedly starved their most talented managers by removing staff, funding, and responsibilities until the managers left – just to play games and be petty.
- Multiple leaders who were protected despite utter incompetence and whose continued actions wreaked havoc on their staff, leading to distress, turnover, and poor customer service.
- Leaders who focus on their own well-being, visibility, and progress, while ignoring the career development needs or even recognizing the contributions of their staff.

You do not have to sacrifice your values and morals to be successful at work politics! Work politics don't have to be corrupt. In fact, some of the most successful managers and leaders use positive, honest politics to both further their career and successfully support their organization in meeting its goals, while still holding on to their values. Furthermore, dishonest politics are often used to protect a small inner circle of people who already have most of the power or advantage. If you are not happy with the current politics at work, engaging in office politics is a critical aspect of developing personal and professional growth, as well as creating positive culture change.

Let's first define what politics really are.

Formal politics refer to how governance structures are set up and how these structures help systems make decisions. Usually, you find these formal politics within more structured, formal, regulated work environments, like federal and state government work. Formal politics can include developing formal policies, passing laws, and promoting and moving forward specific views about how to improve systems.

Informal politics are the underlying invisible structures that also influence decisions. These include how you form alliances, exercise power and authority, protect and advance ideas or goals, and negotiate to access the resources needed, such as information and connections, to aid in decision-making.

Put together, sometimes "politics" can be another way to view the culture of an organization. When you see people spreading rumors, withholding critical information, gossiping, undermining one's credibility (e.g., blaming, interrupting, condescending, patronizing, exposing, teasing), bullying, playing one person against another, and excluding others purposefully from access to information, people, and other resources, you may feel like negative, "dirty", or "dishonest" politics are at play. Keep in mind that not all these actions have bad intent. Sometimes they are an outcome of bad results. For example, if a boss inadvertently pays too much attention to the "people pleasers" or too little attention to good ideas, employees may decide to circumvent current procedures through actions such as these, which are then perpetuated and made worse over time.

Informal politics can occur in a variety of ways and on a continuum. For example, politics includes both hones vs. dishonest interactions to achieve outcomes that are either focused on personal gain vs. community (ie: team, organization, group) gain.

Here is one way to break these informal politics down. In the figure below is a matrix of low to high honest and low to high community.

On the right side you have the high honesty politics. Someone who engages in *honest* community-focused politics would use effective methods of negotiation, persuasion, influence, and advocacy to achieve goals that aligned with the company's mission and values. Laws and policies that are developed to support those efforts would make a

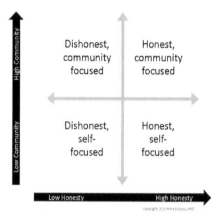

positive difference for many people, through honest means. Someone who engages in *honest* self-focused politics may use those same methods of effective negotiation, persuasion, and influence, but for the purpose of personal promotion or advancement, which may or may not benefit a larger group or community.

On the left side, you have dishonest politics. When you have low honesty (often seen in places that have low psychological safety), it can be played out at either an individual level (self-focused) or community level. So a Vice President of a company who wants to demonstrate that her product line gets the best results might use *dishonest community-focused politics* through coercion and bullying to reach the outcome. In this box, the leader may believe that the "ends justify the means." And if she was just focused on getting a bonus or promotion for herself, then she may engage in *dishonest self-focused politics* by throwing people under the bus or making backroom deals for her own personal gain and power.

Common elements in honest politics are strong positive communication, effective problem-solving skills, developing strong relationships, supporting and advocating for others, and creating effective positive organizational change. It's often the self-focused, dishonest misuse of communication and strategy for personal gain that ruins good politics and are most harmful to people as well as the whole organization.

It's also helpful to have emotional intelligence (the capacity to be aware of, control, and express your emotions, as well as to handle interpersonal relationships judiciously and empathetically) and to create a workplace with psychological safety (an interaction between you and your environment that enables you to be your professional self and speak up without fear of negative consequences to your self-image, status, or career).

In *Millennials' Guide to Workplace Politics*, we teach you proactive strategies to create the self-awareness, emotional intelligence, network, communication skills, problem solving skills – as well as an environment with psychological safety -- to strengthen yourself and your team so you can manage self-focused, dishonest politics better. Given that even the best intentions won't protect you from difficult people, we also discuss reactive strategies to help you address negative politics head-on when needed.

Mira Brancu, PhD
Jennifer Wisdom, PhD MPH ABPP
February 1, 2021

HOW TO USE THIS BOOK

If you've read *Millennials' Guide to Work: What No One Ever Told You About How to Achieve Success and Respect*, or *Millennials' Guide to Management and Leadership: What No One Ever Told You About How to Excel as a Leader*, you know how this works. Millennials' Guides are not books best read cover to cover. We encourage you to review the table of contents and identify a challenge you are currently having or recently experienced. Turn to those pages to start finding a solution!

Each challenge includes a brief description and many possible solutions that you may want to try. Many times, you can see success after trying one option. You'll see some solutions repeated across different challenges because they're likely to be helpful for many problems. For complex challenges, you may want to attempt several interventions at the same time.

It's important to have patience and give the solutions a little bit of time to work. Some ideas that you try won't solve the problem but will make it a little better--that's still success! If you don't feel comfortable trying a solution or if it works partially or not at all, try something else. Some of the solutions are very low risk, such as changing your expectations of the other person. Others can appear more challenging, such as directly discussing a problem with a colleague or negotiating with a competitive colleague. Start with solutions that feel like lower risk to you and work your way up to more challenging solutions.

In this book, we share how to navigate workplace politics. We will provide examples for how to distinguish between proactive and reactive (or defensive) politics and what to do about it. In addition, we have separated the book into three sections: how to take proactive measures, when you need to be reactive, and when to consider letting go or leaving the organization due to an untenable situation. Ideally, you always want to start with setting up as many proactive measures as you can to create the strongest infrastructure for yourself and your organization.

The few basic rules of work will never steer you wrong--especially as managers and leaders:

1. Never say anything bad about anyone at work to anyone at work. (Do your venting at home or with friends.)
2. Write emails and chat messages as if they will be printed in the newspaper, broadcast on social media, used in a court case, or forwarded to others included the person who are talking about (because they might be).
3. Be honest and diplomatic with everyone, including yourself.
4. Be patient. Sometimes people are working on your behalf to make things better and you don't even know it.
5. Be curious about yourself and seek constant self-improvement.
6. Remember that we all have struggles. Be kind and respectful.
7. These skills do not come naturally to most people. That's okay. Practice to get better.
8. Practice healthy skepticism and perspective-taking at work. Not everything can or should be taken at face value. Exploring what other people might be working toward and understanding what their needs are helps you gain greater control of your work life.

As you work through possible solutions, you'll get better at reading situations, responding to people you work with, building networks and connections, and applying solutions effectively to use politics for good. There will sometimes be political situations in which there is a game being played that you don't fully get. Observe, be patient, clarify your own boundaries, and learn. The more you know what you want, the more you'll be able to achieve your goals. If you're not sure what you want, that's okay too--that's a perfect place to be while you're in your 20s and 30s – and even later! The goal of the strategies in this book is to help you develop skills that will serve you well as you continue to move forward at work.

Each of you reading this book is a unique person with talents to share

with the world. Our hope is that this book can make it easier for you to do so. Good luck improving your work life!

Section 1:
Proactive Strategies:
How to Gain Positive Influence to Head off Problems

This book is divided into three sections: Proactive strategies (Section 1) help you set the stage for a positive outcome by guiding you to develop self-awareness, create a strong positive network of allies, and communicate clearly and effectively. When proactive strategies don't work, you can try reactive strategies (Section 2). Proactive strategies usually fall under those "honest politics" that we discussed in the introduction and many often include a community (as compared to a self) focus. We start with the most important proactive strategy of all: self-awareness.

A. Self-Awareness:
How to understand yourself to have greater control in a situation

To successfully navigate complex political landscapes, you need to know what you bring to the table, including your mindset, career goals, and personality traits. You need to know what energizes you. You need to understand what gets you irritated, frustrated, or angry and why that is. Only when you understand these things about yourself will you be most effective. These chapters will provide several tools for how you can get to know yourself better. The more you know yourself, the more control you have in minimizing your potential blind spots, the stronger your political savvy, and the more people will trust you and believe in your work. The hard work of intentional, continual self-reflection is the key that unlocks everything else in this book.

Chapter 1.
How to develop your personal leadership

Understanding yourself within the context of work includes developing a vision for how you want to be seen and how you want to influence and lead others. Self-awareness of these aspects of your work life helps you develop a personal power that helps you better manage forces of power outside yourself. The examples we share here are methods for how to develop an "honest self-focused" political lens and will help you when you expand your perspective to "honest community-focused" politics (see Introduction for more information).

1. **It's a good first step to clarify your values.** Values are statements of what we find important, valuable, or useful. Taking some time to clarify what we authentically value and where we draw the line can be important to guide us as we move forward in our careers. For example, are you committed to honesty, transparency, doing what your boss tells you, the bottom line, all of the above, or something else? What values are important to you? Here's a list you can check out: https://www.threadsculture.com/core-values-examples

2. **It's also helpful to clarify your role in the organization.** This includes your official role, such as in the organization chart and in your job description. It also includes the unofficial roles you may play, such as cheerleader, innovator, truth-teller, or even the "buffer" to protect others. If you're not sure about these unofficial roles, ask trusted colleagues how they see you. You may learn about some roles you fill that are, in fact, unintentional – or maybe unwanted! The goal is to be as aware and intention as you can be about both official and unofficial roles you may carry.

3. **Identify your leadership style, approach, and what areas you feel most or least confident.** Awareness, competence, and confidence are closely connected. The more you are aware of your own leadership approach, the more you can demonstrate confidence that the goals are achievable, that the team can accomplish even more than they think they can, and that you believe in your team, which also

improves your competency. Leaders and managers demonstrate confidence because others on the team look to them for assurance that things are going well, that everything will be okay, and that they are safe. It's important to identify areas in which you don't feel confident, so you can address them, improve your skills, and increase your confidence.

4. **Use who you are and your path to this position as an asset.** Many of us have felt embarrassed about our humble backgrounds, especially when surrounded by people with more impressive college or family connections. Others went to a prep school and Ivy League college. Whatever your path to this position, sharing your journey and struggles with others – and bringing your whole self to work -- can be an inspiration to them to continue to push themselves to excel. In addition, your experiences are unique to you, which makes them your asset. Tap into them when they can lend a new perspective to problem-solving.

5. **Be authentic and diplomatic.** Sometimes people think being "authentic" means they can say whatever occurs to them without regard to others' feelings or perspectives. We recommend instead a diplomatic authenticity, where you speak up and speak out -- in a way that is always professional and respectful, and which reflects who you are. You can share your perspective and concerns in a way that is also thoughtful, intentional, self-reflective, and caring of others' feelings. In fact, this method of being yourself and stating your honest concerns with care and consideration demonstrates great power and influence.

6. **Find opportunities to build your resilience, negotiation skills, networking skills, patience, and communication skills.** Every moment can be a learning opportunity, even the most challenging moments (especially the most challenging moments!). Every political situation, every good boss, every bad boss, every challenging colleague: all are opportunities to learn and improve your skills. We discuss how to build these skills in later chapters.

7. **Like finding opportunities, make opportunities to learn.** Identify technical, interpersonal, and other skills you'd like to improve and set goals. You can learn through targeted mentoring and feedback,

online courses, books, and strategic activities. Time will pass whether you learn or not, so you might as well learn!

8. **Your self-awareness also includes self-care.** If you are burned out, on the edge, or otherwise not doing well, you're not going to be able to manage workplace politics as well as you'd like. Especially as you move up in your organization, ensure you have a self-care regimen that addresses moving your body, sleep, food, and support, however those look for you. Take care of yourself and you'll be better able to do everything!

9. **Your leadership approach will likely change over time.** Be mindful of how your leadership philosophy and approach may change over time and across roles. This is a natural progression, and your awareness of these changes will help you assess what works best and what adjustments you need to make.

10. **Learn more about yourself and your management and leadership style.** Check out our books *Millennials' Guide to Work* and *Millennials' Guide to Management and Leadership* for more about work environments, building self-awareness and developing your own leadership style.

See also:

Chapter 2: Tools That Build Self-Awareness
Chapter 3: Addressing Limiting Internal Barriers And Mindsets
Chapter 7: How To Become Indispensable

Chapter 2.
Tools that build self-awareness

Knowing yourself well is the most fundamental building block of navigating complex politics. Did you know we all make assumptions about people and situations all the time? The human brain likes to create order from chaos and simplify confusing or overwhelming information by categorizing people and things. This means sometimes we miss critical information in our environment to make it more manageable. For example, some of us tend to assume bad intent of others, even when there isn't any, whereas some of us may naively assume the best in everyone and miss a healthy dose of skepticism or cross-checking. These assumptions we routinely make can sabotage our best efforts. That's why it's important to catch and question the assumptions we make in complex situations, slow ourselves down, and try to gather more information to make sure our brain isn't steering us in the wrong direction. Here are some resources and techniques you can use to improve your ability to do this.

1. **To better prepare to approach complex situations, you must identify what is within your awareness and what may be out of your awareness (blind spots).** Do you ever find yourself feeling like other people in the meeting seem to know more background about the topic than you do? That might be a blind spot (and it could also be politics at play!). How about times when you realize you have some unique knowledge or experience that no one else does? That may be a hidden opportunity to showcase a unique strength! How can you figure out what is unique to you, what is an awareness you share with others, and what you are missing that is a blind spot for you? Read the rest of these tips to identify some methods to try.

2. **Coaching.** There are many types of coaches available to help with self-awareness and performance building. Formal coaches (i.e., those who have received formal training in coaching and may charge a fee for their services) include life coaches, career coaches, executive coaches, and many more. Coaches help their clients define, explore, and reach specific goals. Some leaders engage in executive coaching

services to help them onboard into new roles and navigate many new complex situations, seek and prepare for higher level promotions, and navigate ongoing complex challenges as the need arises. Mentors, supervisors, and peers can sometimes become great informal coaches, too.

3. **Consulting.** Consulting is similar in some ways to coaching except consultants are specifically sought out for their subject matter expertise and expert advice. Consultants usually provide solutions and guidance by assessing the situation directly (often using surveys) and sometimes also implementing those solutions or training others to do so, such as facilitating a strategic planning meeting or a team development workshop.

4. **Mentoring.** Mentoring is like coaching and consulting in that it is driven by the client's identified goals. Like consulting, it involves an expert sharing their knowledge and experience in a specific area that the mentee is seeking. Within an organization, mentoring is available for free. However, access to a good, appropriate mentor might sometimes be hard to find. Sometimes you can find good mentors outside an organization, and in some cases (like if you own a business), you can find paid business mentorships. Most people benefit from having multiple mentors to access more perspectives and for different needs.

5. **Supervision.** Supervision is kind of like mentorship but there is a different power dynamic there because supervisors officially evaluate your work performance; have the power to hire, fire, or promote; and direct the work (tasks, caseload, flow) of their employees. Supervisors serve a great role in providing you with critical feedback about your performance and how to strengthen your skillset (see Chapters 19-21 on giving and receiving feedback). Employees often assume their supervisors want to also serve as mentors to them. This is sometimes the case, but not always! Having your supervisor also serving as your mentor can be complicated because you may be seeking their approval while also trying to be vulnerable enough to improve your skills. Or you might be interested in being promoted or moving to a
new department that your supervisor might not want to have happen. Seeking (additional) mentorship outside of the supervisory

relationship is therefore wise for many reasons. That said, past supervisors can sometimes turn into great future mentors, so stay in touch with the supervisors who demonstrate an interest in your career.

6. **Therapy.** Unlike coaching, therapy focuses on treating mental health conditions, such as depression and anxiety through specific behavioral interventions. Like coaching, these interventions have the capacity to help clients ultimately reach their highest potential, but by first and foremost addressing a mental health challenge that may interfere with reaching certain goals.

7. **Education.** Seek opportunities to continue learning through both formal (academic) and informal (e.g., reading) mechanisms, within your organization and outside of it. Create a diverse portfolio for learning so that you are not receiving all your information from only one source. Your continued education should include increasing understanding about yourself through resources such as those recommended at the end of this book.

8. **Assessments.** Consultants, coaches, and therapists often use formal assessments like personality inventories, "strength finders", and leadership style profilers to help you learn more about yourself. In addition, there are free online assessments also available. Do your homework to identify credible sources for research-supported assessments and then take some every few years to learn more about yourself and how you have developed professionally.

9. **Cultural Awareness.** Seek ways to learn how history and culture may influence how you perceive yourself and the world. Some of this may come out in supervision, therapy, or more general education, but some may not. For example, messages like "I have to keep my head down," "Self-promotion is selfish," "I can never really become a leader," "I don't belong here," and "I need to be the provider of my family" are all messages that are rooted in gender and cultural stereotypes that have been passed down from one generation to another. Catch and challenge yourself when you make disparaging remarks about your future potential or when you believe someone who says these things to you, and then seek to clarify for yourself what myths need to be dispelled and what you want to achieve.

See also:

Chapter 1: How To Develop Your Personal Leadership
Chapter 3: Addressing Limiting Internal Barriers And Mindsets
Chapter 21: How To Gracefully Accept Feedback And Apply
Effectively

Chapter 3.
Addressing limiting internal barriers and mindsets

There are many systemic barriers in organizations that we may not have any control over. However, developing our self-awareness will help us identify internal barriers that we DO have control over. These internal barriers include mindsets that cause us to become stuck thinking or believing in only one way and can trap us into creating more problems for ourselves. Here are some examples of internal barriers worthy of taking note and addressing.

1. **Catch and adjust self-defeating thoughts and limiting beliefs.** Simple words that imply a strong direction or black-and-white thinking, such as "can't," "must," and "should" can limit our behaviors and impact. Changing these words can significantly impact how effective we are in achieving successful outcomes. For example: Self-defeating thought: "ALL politics are all dirty - I will NEVER engage in them." Alternative: "Despite how much I hate politics, organizations are political by nature and require my engagement, so I will TRY to engage in politics, but in a way that feels right to me: honest, thoughtful, and proactive whenever possible."

2. **Catch and adjust self-sabotaging beliefs.** Self-sabotaging beliefs hold you back or keep you from engaging in activities you need to do to succeed. Here are some examples for how to catch and adjust them: Self-sabotaging belief: "Self-promotion is just for people who think they are better than others. I just need to keep my nose down and work hard, and I'll be noticed for my work and be promoted." This belief assumes you are being watched closely, even though supervisors are focused on many other things. It also assumes that people in power will automatically notice your achievements without you having to communicate anything about how you are contributing to the organization in significant ways. Self-supporting alternative: "I recognize that my leaders are very busy,

and they might appreciate hearing from me occasionally about the work I am doing to support the company's mission. I will create a better communication plan to make sure they are kept abreast of work that they may want to know about."

3. **Face fears about being seen as incompetent.** When we allow our fear of being perceived as incompetent to take over, we sometimes develop bigger problems such as perfectionism and "analysis paralysis" in which we overthink and underperform. Some also call this fear "imposter syndrome." These fears can lead some people to even miss deadlines and procrastinate, which could lead to them being perceived as less competent because they can't deliver the work on time. Success comes from being willing to try, ask for what you need, and knowing it might not work out. If you try, there is a chance. If you don't, there is no chance. Practice asking and trying as often as you can. Learn to recognize when there are institutional barriers holding you back from trying, as compared to your own personal barriers. See also Chapters 1 and 2 on how to understand yourself.

4. **Face any internal need to be liked and accepted that is interfering with strong decision-making.** Sometimes a consensus can't be reached. Sometimes, there will be a few people on a team who will not want to go along with a decision. Practice having conversations in which you develop healthy constructive conflict rather than avoiding conflict altogether.

5. **Learn how to tolerate conflict.** Not all conflict is bad. In the highest performing workplaces, teams and their leaders have a strong ability to engage in healthy disagreement to problem-solve. The ability to tolerate conflict in order to provide tough feedback is also a critical leadership skill. Positive personal and professional growth will be significantly stunted if you do not build this skill.

6. **Develop an "It's Just Business" mindset.** By this we mean, be careful about making assumptions about the intent of others as something personal to you. For example, do not assume a conflict or disagreement is personal. If you experience your emotions running high or that you are feeling defensive, first take some time to process where the defensiveness is coming from (see self-awareness activities above). Each conversation includes both a

process and a content aspect. Break it down to understand these two pieces better. For example, "I understand you want budget details because you feel the budget cuts are not fair [content]. At the same time, I am having a very strong reaction to your tone [process], because it sounds like you don't trust that we value your work. As you know, my focus has always been on equitable and fair distribution for the organization. The budget decisions are not personal."

7. **Identify when your fear of being labeled or judged is interfering with your achievement goals.** A critical principle of being successful is reducing your concern about being labeled as "ambitious", "intimidating", "suck up", or "power-grabber." If your efforts are truly done with integrity (see Chapters 4-9 on power and influence), these negative judgments are more about the person doing the judging than they are about you. These attributions are sometimes also applied more often to women or other people from marginalized groups. See Section 2 for how to respond to comments that become toxic or threaten the psychological safety of you or your team.

8. **Identify your implicit biases and practice challenging them.** This is one of the hardest tasks but so important for effectively navigating workplace politics effectively. Implicit (sometimes called unconscious) bias happens automatically – we aren't usually aware when it's happening - and affects how we think about and interact with other people. Nobody is free from having implicit bias. Here are three best practices to help you challenge your implicit biases: (1) Get to know the people you work with. The better you know people on a personal level, the more likely you can question automatic assumptions. (2) Ask for feedback routinely (see Chapters 19-21 on giving and receiving feedback). (3) Notice, pause, and reflect when someone tells you they feel offended, or they look distressed in response to something you said. See also Chapters 1 on how to understand yourself.

9. **Identify confirmation bias and practice questioning it.** Like implicit bias, confirmation bias is something we all do: seeking out and preferring information that confirms our current perception, beliefs, and views. For example, seeing everything an employee you

really like does as positive, and everything an employee you don't care for as negative. If you find yourself selectively using some information and ignoring other information that doesn't fit with your current understanding, you may be guilty of confirmation bias. Unfortunately, if we only use information that confirms what we already believe, we are likely to keep making the same decisions, instead of the best decisions based on the full picture.

10. **You can find out much more about developing your self-awareness by reading about emotional intelligence.** See the Further Reading section for some suggestions.

See also:

Chapter 2: Tools That Build Self-Awareness
Chapter 6: What Are Power And Influence?
Chapter 20: How To Ask For (Useful) Feedback

B. Power and Influence

Understanding the flow of power and influence and how to garner it is a critical component for career advancement that cannot be overlooked. How do you get heard? How do you get a seat at the table when you are not in a leadership role? How can you influence decisions and directions to make an impact even if you do not have an official leadership title? The answer lies in understanding the organization's strengths, weaknesses, untapped opportunities, and threats; historical changes; who has and receives power, authority, and responsibility; what visible structures people employees follow (or don't); and how the organization works (or doesn't). The next few chapters will focus on learning what you need to know and how to learn it.

Chapter 4.
How to gain a broader perspective about your organization's history

Learning more about the history of your organization can help you get some perspective that informs current staff behaviors and attitudes. The goal of this research is to have a better understanding of formal and informal aspects of how an organization works, how people communicate with each other, how people resolve conflict, and where friction points are.

Below is a list of potential information you may want to gather about your organization. Keep in mind these questions are rarely asked directly - and rarely answered sufficiently by others - because workplace politics are often "unspoken". Instead find ways to gather information indirectly, for example, by observing, indirectly exploring how to get a project started and approved, or by asking advice about your own career decisions.

1. When, by whom, and how was the organization founded?
2. How has the mission changed over time (if at all) and why?
3. What are the organization's values? Have they changed over time and why?
4. What crises has the organization experienced and how were those managed?
5. How has the succession of leaders happened?
6. What have been consistent challenges over time for the organization?
7. Who has power and how did they achieve that power?
8. Who gets promoted and why?
9. What does the formal organizational chart look like (including a Board of Directors, if applicable)? Does it match your understanding of how work is aligned in reality?
10. What are job descriptions for key positions? How did those descriptions come to be?

11. How is the organization geographically distributed? Is there one location that appears to be stronger than others? Are some employees more likely to be hired from some of the locations than others (e.g., due to physical distance and proximity to higher levels of power and influence)?
12. What are the organization's financial priorities? What is funded and not funded?
13. What is the decision-making structure and how does that compare to the formal positions on the organizational chart?
14. How does the company manage recruitment, orientation, training, professional development, supervision, health, and other aspects related to employees? Is it transparent?
15. What is the scope of policies and procedures and how well are they communicated and followed?

See also:

Chapter 5: How To Understand Power Through Relationships And Communication Flow
Chapter 7: How To Become Indispensable
Chapter 12: How To Increase Your Visibility Through Strategic Communication

Chapter 5.
How to understand power through relationships and communication flow

In addition to understanding the *history* of the development of the organization and its structure (Chapter 4), it is also critical to understand power and influence from the perspective of *relationships and communication flow*. This is much harder to assess as it's not always obvious. For example, policies may be developed and communicated through typical memo and email channels, but how they are used and applied in real life by those in power positions might be quite different. Assume nothing. Instead do your research by asking others and closely observing.

1. **Evaluate the internal attitudes between teams and groups in the organization.** Do certain policies or procedures create more negative conflict? What appears to be influencing these attitudes? Are people aligned on the policies and procedures across different departments? Are people aligned with the company's vision and goals? Does one team get more recognition more often than others? When there is disagreement between departments or teams, who "wins" or gets supported more often?
2. **Evaluate internal and external relationships.** Internal groups include employees, leaders, committees. They can be formal (following the formal organizational structure and job titles) or informal (functional interdisciplinary task groups). External groups include customers, competitive organizations, employees, legislative bodies, and community groups. What are the attitudes and relationships between these groups around policies, procedures, or other communications? Has it always been like this? Do certain changes or challenges create different reactions? When there is noticeable friction between groups, who brings everyone together to help them discuss, analyze, and align?
3. **Evaluate the level to which communication about decisions are transparent and open to discussion.** An organizational culture that has more transparency, invites open discussion, and provides

explanations of decisions often has less complicated and problematic politics. One that is "hard to crack" in understanding the flow of communication, how decisions are made, and back-door discussions has a much more complicated and often problematic political system. Beware of "false transparency" in which leaders say one thing but their actions consistently tell a different story. This is the kind of culture that falls under the "hard to crack/back-door" category. Crack the code by focusing on the pattern of the actions and what story that tells.

4. **Assess whether and how often there are opportunities to discuss and provide input about decisions.** Are there opportunities to hear about early pre-decision discussions and offer input? How often? If so, does it appear that feedback is incorporated into final decisions and explanations are provided for why or why not? Ideally the level to which these opportunities occur does not land on an extreme: too much time spent listening, explaining, and revising decisions based on a lot of feedback can slow down a process unnecessarily and can create a lot of frustration, whereas too little can degrade trust and create employee disengagement or low morale.

5. **Evaluate who is invited to partake in decision-making.** Those who are invited have the most power in the organization. Does it make sense why they are invited (e.g., they have a position of decision-making authority, they are high performers with future leadership potential) or does it seem like there may be a degree of favoritism for individuals who do not otherwise have a decision-making position nor demonstrated value/impact? Are there strong external influences on the decision-making process by individuals that are not part of the organization?

6. **Evaluate the level of connection between the policies and their implementation.** Are decisions and policies communicated clearly and available through written and verbal methods, but then not followed? To what degree? No organization is perfect in their ability to flawlessly implement an ideal set of policies or decisions, but the greater the gap, the greater the concern that they are not practicing what they preach, which creates more political landmines to potentially have to navigate.

7. **Assess how employees perceive decisions and communications.** Do employees generally follow decisions or policies? Do they appreciate the communication? Do they attend routine all-staff meetings to learn more about upcoming changes? Sparsely attended meetings or poorly attended-to policies might communicate a greater level of disengagement or mistrust.

8. **Evaluate the level of chaos and confusion after policies or decisions are communicated.** The greater the chaos and confusion, the more likely that there are problems with executing and developing sound implementation procedures, or simply having enough clarity and alignment communicated. A leadership team that cannot align and execute in these ways makes it harder for the rest of the organization to succeed.

9. **If you want to learn more about organizational assessment,** check out the work of Harry Levinson in the For Further Reading section.

See also:

Chapter 4: How To Gain A Broader Perspective About Your Organization's History
Chapter 6: What Are Power And Influence?
Chapter 11: How To Communicate To Build Strong, Healthy Teams

Chapter 6.
What are power and influence?

Social psychologists John French and Bertram Raven described 6 sources of power. Some of these sources are bestowed upon leaders by their official title and formal role in the organization, such as CEO, Director, or Vice President. But sometimes the lines of power and influence go beyond those who hold those official positions of authority. For example, Expert power (based on knowledge), Referential power (based on knowing others in power, such as through networking relationships), and Informational power (based on having information others may not), can be developed regardless of title or position. Brandon & Seldman (2004), in their book *Survival of the Savvy*, describe the power of ideas (the substance of the work) vs power of people (position, image, perception, relationship-based). Regardless of type, any source of power can be used with integrity or can be abused. If used well, you can strengthen your ability to get work done more effectively and with integrity, as follows.

1. **Learn about industry trends from information provided outside your organization.** This can include mainstream business articles, leadership podcasts, and other mechanisms. It will provide you with insight into what your leaders might be reading and the language they use to describe work and outcomes. It can help you connect and translate your work to this language. It can also help you learn what you might be missing or inspire you to work in a different way.
2. **Track the news.** Business, financial, and other industry-specific news can provide insight about events that may impact an entire industry and how decisions are made about that impact.
3. **Talk to experts.** This goes a step beyond passive learning into more interactive learning. You can learn from experts within and outside your organization to better understand what works, what may not work, and learn how experts think.
4. **Read company policies, regulations, and memos and attend all-company meetings.** Having a strong understanding of company policies, regulations, and how they are communicated can provide a

lot of information about how well a company sticks to and can explain decisions and changes. You can identify when there are discrepancies between policies or in how information is communicated. You can better understand the communication of a change when you have read the original source. And you can provide creative solutions to problems when you have gathered information about how different policies work together and how they are communicated.

5. **Become an expert.** Using the information above as well as other knowledge you gain, you can eventually develop the kind of knowledge and skills others seek out to solve complex problems. Demonstrating solid judgment based on that knowledge and skillset helps you demonstrate your value and gain respect and trust in your work as being of value to the company.

6. **Learn and stay abreast of the organization's strategic goals and priorities.** Understanding strategic goals and priorities helps you know how your work is valued by that organization and how to explain and translate your work into the language of what is valued. This information is often made available at all-company meetings, in company messaging, and sometimes also publicly available depending on the type of company.

7. **Treat people with kindness and support them and get known for it.** This sounds like an unexpected way to garner power, but Referent power is all about becoming known, liked, and trusted. If people in power get to know you, appreciate your work, and trust your work, they are more likely to include you in more opportunities, which eventually leads you to gain power related to your work with them. Make sure you can gain this with honesty and integrity, rather than by manipulating others into liking and trusting you, though.

8. **Ensure that the work you communicate is supported by well-researched information, not just opinion.** The power of ideas, as well as Expert and Informational power, are developed and maintained when others believe you have done your due diligence to gather needed information to support your recommendations or claims. Without this, if you are not in a position of formal authority, this type of power will be quickly lost due to loss of trust. Use and refer to data to support your ideas whenever possible.

See also:

Chapter 7.
How to become indispensable

Becoming indispensable means being seen as a highly valued employee and leader who gets things done effectively and has the political savvy to make things happen successfully within the organization. This is aligned with developing an "honest community-focused" type of political savvy (See Introduction for more on this). Let's see how employees become indispensable...

1. **Be the one who fills "structural holes" in the organization.** Originally developed within social network research by Ronald Stuart Burt, "structural holes" are gaps in organizations where people typically don't work together but have untapped complementary sources of information. If you can serve as the liaison or lynchpin that connects them, you are creating relationships and structures that addresses important gaps for the organization and help them all be more successful. For example, you have a relationship with the IT department and learn they just developed a web portal to track productivity but are looking for ways to evaluate the effectiveness of some of their work. You also have a relationship with someone in the research department and find out they are looking for a way to track their own productivity. Bring them together and offer ideas for how they can help each other and BAM! You might have just created opportunities for all and better served the organization.

2. **Understand how different departments or groups in the organization work.** You can proactively become a critical piece to problem-solving if you know how different groups can come together, break down silos, and leverage each other's knowledge to achieve results. Note that this method requires significant time to build relationships and knowledge. But be careful here: avoid misusing this power so that you do not become the lynchpin of disaster! One of our well-intentioned colleagues, who has a knack for problem-solving, recalls a situation in which she became overly involved in helping a group of people solve a problem that was not hers to solve. Unfortunately, it became even more complicated after

she got in the middle of it. Looking back, she realized it would have been better to connect the individuals having the conflict to encourage them to solve it together, but without her getting in the middle.

3. **Consider how you'd like to be perceived, and then work on that.** How do you want to be seen: as a striver? A helper? A go-getter? A calm neutral party? Think about how you'd like to be perceived and then do your own observation to see how you're seen. You may want to ask trusted others how they see you.

4. **Find opportunities to offer support and solutions for those in power...** Listen and pay close attention to their burdens and pain points. They often share these in meetings, in company emails, and other situations. Think about how you can apply your experience and expertise to be of service to reduce that burden. Offer solutions that connect their spoken and unspoken burdens that you identified for which your expertise matches. For example, saying, "Hey boss, I keep hearing the CEO talk about improving our vertical integration, do you need help with figuring out what we need to do about it within our department?"

5. **...But avoid offering too much unsolicited advice.** Offering unsolicited solutions to those in power can be useful when provided in moderation and when dialogue appears welcomed. Think about the right time and place. Start with appreciation for what has already been done and an invitation for further dialogue, such as "I really appreciated what you shared at the staff meeting the other day and have been thinking a lot about it within the context of the recent strategic plan you shared. Are you looking for any help or support with it?"

6. **Serve as a "buffer" for leaders you admire and trust.** Offer to take an unwanted task off your leader's hands. If your leader takes you up on your offer, agree on how you will be of service. Set up a system to report back routinely and/or ideally demonstrate through visible action how you are addressing that need for this leader. Here's an example of what this looks like: "I heard this task will take a lot of work - a lot of spreadsheets, calling, and uploading weekly reports.... Would you like any help with that? I'm happy to help - it would certainly be a good learning opportunity for me."

7. **Reinforce organizational goals and your alignment with them.** When speaking with leaders within the organization about a new goal, idea, or suggestion you have, try to tie it back to how it aligns with the organizational priorities and goals. For example, you could say, "I was thinking about that goal for increasing our focus on diversity and inclusion. Can I share how I'm thinking about addressing it and let me know if I'm on track with being aligned with this goal from your perspective?"

8. **Get a seat at the table … and then help those at the table.** Have you heard the recommendation to "Get a seat at the table" and wondered "Which table? How?" Deciding which table and how is important as it can make a difference in whether your work is ultimately recognized as valuable to the organization and implemented. Observe and identify the various meetings, committees, workgroups, task forces and other "tables" that are happening within the organization and which you might be best suited for, given your skill set. If there are several options, choose those comprised of the highest level of leaders with decision-making capability, power, and influence. Being at these decision-making tables can help you make a greater potential impact, and thus become more indispensable for the valuable support you can provide to these groups. Keep in mind that unless you were invited only for the purpose of taking notes, try to volunteer for roles where you are seen as a leader, not simply a note-taker (if people take turns doing this, it's not a problem, however).

9. **Volunteer for leadership roles that are undesirable to others.** Committees and workgroups work only if there is someone directing the work, moving it forward, delegating tasks, compiling, and reporting out information, and making decisions. But senior leaders rarely have time for these tasks. Your willingness to volunteer, AND to be successful in getting the job done, will undoubtably increase visibility in your value. Prioritize opportunities for which you can (1) serve in a leadership capacity, (2) increase visibility of your abilities, and (3) maximize your impact in helping the company succeed.

When possible, avoid becoming the "room parent" (i.e., clean-up, party planner, and other non-decision-making jobs). These are fine if everyone chips in and takes turns, but not okay if that's the only job you end up doing each time because you will eventually be seen as non-essential to the decision-making process.

10. **Create documents that help improve work efficiencies and employee effectiveness.** Saving the company time, money, and aggravation is always a win. If you notice routine workflows or tasks in which employees keep asking the same things (e.g., "How do we do this again?"), the same work is constantly being done in different ways by different people, or other inefficient or ineffective ways of doing routine work, first gather information about the history of that decision. If there doesn't seem to be a very good reason and it appears there is interest in improving this workflow, offer to create a Standard Operating Procedure (SOP) or "How-To" guide and then serve as a trainer or auditor to ensure consistency.

11. **Offer to be the researcher for a project.** Volunteer to research a topic and summarize best practices, recent trends, options, pros and cons, etc. These are arduous tasks that are highly valued (when done well).

See also:

Chapter 1: How To Develop Your Personal Leadership
Chapter 8: How To Build Alliances And Allies Through Strategic Networking
Chapter 12: How To Increase Your Visibility Through Strategic Communication

Chapter 8.
How to build alliances and allies through strategic networking

Gone are the days when one person can single-handedly create something new and take sole claim for that innovation. When done well, a team-based approach usually leads to better and more innovative products and outcomes. In addition to developing and working with teams, developing partnerships to serve specific needs also supports great outcomes. Here are some ways to do that:

1. **Serve on boards, committees, task forces, etc.** These types of teams are often comprised of members from different parts of the organization. Your willingness to help and develop positive relationships across the organization can make you a valuable team player, as well as becoming adept at seeking out the right people to help with future needs.

2. **Create cross-functional connections inside the organization.** Connect with and develop relationships with people outside of your team and department. The easiest way to do this is to identify and engage in collaborative projects. Remember that any new relationship takes time to build. Put in the same amount of time into building your strategic relationships as you would into any worthy high-impact project – and be successful! (Consider how you can fill "structural holes" described in *Chapter 7: How to become indispensable.*)

3. **Build strategic relationships and partnerships outside the organization as well as inside.** Who should you know? Who should know YOU? Who's work touches on yours or could help enhance your own? Who would be interested and want to know about your work? Find ways to connect with them and share interests, ideas, and potential involvement. Focus both on the strategic relationships your company would benefit from, through you, as well as those you would benefit from professionally. This can include serving on internal boards, committee, and task forces (see #1) and also getting to know professionals across different organizations.

4. **For each of project you own that may have an important organizational impact, evaluate who needs to know about it and in what way.** Consider:
   - Who needs to be involved at the earliest stages of the project?
   - Who needs to be kept updated of the progress along the way?
   - Are there experts who could serve in an advisory or mentorship capacity on this project?
   - What resources do you need and are there stakeholders who could help support or provide those resources?
   - Are there stakeholders who can help with informing the alignment of this project with other larger organizational efforts?
   - Are there stakeholders who can help the project gain greater visibility?
5. **Cultivate advocates and champions who would support your work in meetings when you're not there.** Identify and cultivate relationships you can trust who can support and advocate for you and your work when you are not there. Do the same for them. This will ensure that the work you and your advocates are doing is not getting lost, ignored, or unfairly dismissed when you are not present to communicate about it directly.
6. **Publicly acknowledge the achievements of your peers and direct reports.** Recognize the situations in which you can advocate or speak up for others. Think about what you appreciate when someone else publicly recognizes your good work and make sure to do the same for others. This is good role modeling and sets the tone for others to follow similarly. In addition, many of those people whom you support in this way will remember this and likely do the same for you when needed in the future.
7. **Find ways to help people outside of your team.** Listen to and identify ways you might be able to help others across the organization that are outside your immediate sphere of influence but within your sphere of competence. One caveat: Be careful not to stretch yourself too thin or lose sight of your primary responsibility to your own team – people will lose trust in you if you are spread so thin you can't deliver on your commitments -- in the timeline they need from you.

8. **Keep others updated about the work you do.** You never know who might need your expertise, support, influence, or insights. Make it a habit to try to share what you are working on with others, so they keep you in mind when opportunities arise.

See also:

Chapter 9.
The downside of gaining power and influence

Even when you gain power and influence with integrity in positive, proactive, honest ways, there are going to be some downsides you will need to know about and manage.

1. **Recognize that you can't trust just anyone.** Yes, this is a negative-sounding statement. But it is the reality, especially in situations with competing priorities and resources. People don't always have your needs in mind, nor prioritize your needs over their own. The more influence and power you gain, the more important it is to build trust. It's also important to know how to evaluate how well you can trust others to not misuse or abuse your relationship with them. Some might compete with you or use you as an opportunity to further their own careers. Track how people treat you and what they say to keep evaluating how well you can trust those around you to have your back. Remember to keep working hard to be trustworthy yourself. Positive, honest politics means you gain power and influence through ongoing trust-building.

2. **You might lose friendships.** As you gain power and influence, you may have peers who experience envy, anger, loss, or even betrayal toward your increasing power and influence. This could be due to feeling like they were better for the job you got, fear it will change your relationship (e.g., if you become their supervisor), or for other reasons. This is complicated and sometimes messy terrain to navigate. At every level of your career in an organization, keep in mind that your relationships might change. Have compassion and understanding for these changes. Keep your work friendships as professional as possible from the beginning, knowing that you or your peers might someday be in the boss position. A positive, healthy relationship with clear boundaries will be important when that happens.

3. **Your potential risk for breaking others' trust increases.** As you gain power and influence, your words will carry more weight than before. Don't be cavalier with your words. Recognize the power of your off-

hand comments. For example, you might want to still have the same playful, joking, open communication you always had with colleagues. Or you might want to talk through your decision-making process openly with others with the same level of past candor. While your intention may be good (e.g., wanting to be open, transparent, and approachable), given the greater impact you may have, your words may be shared with others who are not in the room and even turned into unnecessary gossip, worry, or competition. How much information makes sense to spread broadly? Ask yourself along the way, "What purpose am I serving by sharing this information?"

4. **You may lose opportunities to engage in social activities in the same way.** As you gain power and influence, people will see you differently. That means if you continue to go out to bars or other social gatherings, you might lose respect if you engage in activities that blur the lines between your new role and your past life. Alternatively, you might send the message that you will give preferential treatment to those with whom you socialize outside of work because you know them better and prefer their company over others. To maintain trust, respect, and fairness, you may need to either curtail some of these activities or maintain the same professional relationship in those settings as you would at work. Ask yourself, "Would I say or do this at work? If someone took a picture of this scene and shared it with my boss or a newspaper, would I be worried about losing my professional reputation?"

5. **There will be people who want to take you down.** We know this sounds harsh, but it is a reality you can't completely escape. As hard as you work on developing healthy, positive, supportive work relationships, there might still be people who will do anything in their power to take you down. Do not assume it's personal but do be ready for it. Section 2 will describe more about what to look for and how to manage these situations.

6. **There will be people who want to tag along.** As your status, power and influence elevates, there will be people who will try to attach themselves to you to personally benefit from your success. They may seem friendly and interested in getting to know you, but their interest in your work is purely selfish. You can identify them by signs such as: (a) They never previously expressed interest in your

work until you got a promotion; (b) They ask many specific questions about your work and who you know, followed by a request for you to introduce them to others in power, put in a good word for them, or get them on an important committee without having worked to establish a mutually trusting relationship with you; (c) They give you many compliments you feel you haven't earned from them as a way to ingratiate themselves to you; or (d) they try to associate with you in any context that allows them to gain visibility or take credit for a contribution they had a minimal hand in (i.e., it's about gaining recognition rather than about helping with the work).

7. **You will need to keep proving yourself to others for a while.** In each new higher-level position or higher professional status, and even in new settings with new people (e.g., new committees you serve on) you may need to keep proving your value and worth. If you are a member of a visible minority (e.g., racial, ethnic, gender, disability), you are probably already familiar with this experience as a constant – and this is further compounded if you are a member of multiple visible minority status groups (e.g., Black women). Don't face it alone - develop and maintain strong strategic allies and alliances to combat this.

8. **Being in a leadership role can be lonely.** The higher your leadership role or status, the harder it is to identify a trusted, objective support person or team to talk about work concerns. It may also be harder to receive accurate feedback when you make mistakes because people might feel they have to agree with you or are afraid to tell you the truth. Many leaders have a coach, mentor, and/or therapist as part of their external support team to explore concerns (see Chapter 2 for when to use each of these). Identify who you need on your support team.

See also:

Chapter 2: Tools That Build Self-Awareness
Chapter 8: How To Build Alliances And Allies Through Strategic Networking
Chapter 10: How To Communicate Credibility And Trust

C: Communicating

Communication includes (1) daily positive, proactive communication for the purpose of strengthening relationships and teams, (2) strategic communication for the purpose of sharing a message effectively and exerting influence, and (3) having difficult conversations for the purpose of effectively managing conflict. Each of these will be addressed within certain identified contexts and situations in the following chapters.

Chapter 10.
How to communicate credibility and trust

Whether for the purpose of strengthening relationships, exerting influence, or effectively managing conflict, there are some foundational skills that will help you convey that you and your work can be trusted and is credible. These are the building blocks:

1. **Trust is a multi-dimensional experience that requires constant assessment and vigilance.** Trusting relationships take years to build, whether in your personal or work life. In addition, it is multi-dimensional. For example, in your personal life, you can trust some people with your money, but you may not trust those same people to take care of your children. You can trust other people with your children, but not with your personal worries. The same is true at work. Whenever you seek to develop strategic relationships, keep this principle in mind and allow yourself the time necessary to continually test and evaluate the strength and type of trust you have in others. They will appreciate your thoughtfulness in wanting to develop a trusting relationship which also helps you gain respect, dependability, and credibility.

2. **Recognize you, too, are liable to break others' trust in you.** Just as you are wisely evaluating how much you trust others, they are doing the same with you (or should be). Trust is a two-way street. Remember to demonstrate consistently what you can (and should) be trusted with. Work hard to build others' trust in you. Trust takes a long time to build, but can be undone quickly, for example after just one attempt at betrayal. Watch for your pitfalls (see Chapters 1-3 on Self Awareness) and communicate your commitment to earn other's trust.

3. **Try to keep your language and emotions balanced.** There are two ends of the communication spectrum to consider. On one end is tentative, apologetic, self-discounting, vague, and ambivalent language. On the other end is threatening, abusive, blaming, and exaggerated language. Unless there is a strategic and purposeful reason to present your case with stronger language, it's usually more

effective to convey confidence, clarity, and understanding when the message is not confounded with extreme language or emotion. Here are examples of the difference between each of these: (1) Tentative, apologetic language sounds like this: "I'm sorry to bother you with this but is there any chance we can move forward with that project? If not, it's okay, I understand." (2) Threatening, blaming or exaggerated language sounds like this: "What do you mean we can't do this project? Clearly nobody here wants to do any meaningful work – why did we even collect that data if the executives have no interest in moving forward??" (3) Confident, clear, understanding language sounds like this: "If I am hearing correctly, you're saying that we don't have all the data to move forward with the project as it is currently written. That's a good point – we certainly don't. Since we do have enough data to support the first phase of this project, what do you think about starting with that?" One strategic and purposeful reason to speak using more emotion (yet still clear and unapologetic), however, is when you are seeking to address toxic behaviors (see *Section 2: Reactive Strategies: When things go south*).

4. **Treat all colleagues using a consistent communication style even if your leadership role or style changes.** You will lose trust quickly if your communication style changes from one person to the next or from one role you take on to the next. Keep it professional across all people and contexts, even with colleagues you might perceive as more like friends. Be especially careful not to offer preferential treatment of past/current friends – it will create unwanted problems over time. This does not mean you must be emotionally cold and shut everyone out. You can be warm and engaging, or any other style that is natural to you. But if you find yourself feeling compelled to gossip, share confidential information, or communicate a preference for one person over another, people will lose confidence and trust in you. One of our colleagues shared with us, "I learned a hard lesson one time that even listening to others complaining and trying to be supportive to the person can bite you when they turn around and say 'and she agrees with me!'" Similarly, watch your non-verbal communication. One of the authors (MB) learned this with an employee who would often complain to her

about other people without checking out his assumptions. She would nod as he talked to show that she was listening and cared about his concerns. Over time, however, she realized he misinterpreted her nodding to mean that she agreed and took his side. To correct this, she reduced the nodding and instead spoke up more often to ask clarifying questions to help him check out his assumptions and send the message that she needed more information. She then used this method with everyone, which helped the outcome match the intent of her communication: showing care and respect while maintaining professionalism and not taking sides. Some friends might not appreciate your professional tone but will respect it if they are true friends.

5. **Aim to communicate a message that your work is focused on aligning with organizational goals.** Sometimes that means you cannot meet individual needs. Explain this clearly to others, for example: "I know this was really important to you. But I also had to think about how this change you are requesting might affect everyone who might be in the same situation. I need to think about what precedent any of my decisions will set and the policies required that could fit all similar requests. After evaluating it I just couldn't make an exception here. Let's think about another way I can support you without creating a larger cascade of changes we can't currently make."

6. **Maintain your work relations as professional as possible.** You spend the large proportion of your day at work, and this means you develop meaningful relationships with your colleagues. However, as noted above, gaining power and influence makes these relationships highly complicated to navigate. Keeping all your work relationships as professional as possible helps minimize the potential damage. This means finding a balance between joining your colleagues in and out of work for purely work-related celebrations while minimizing over-socializing in non-work-related ways. In other words, work hard to maintain healthy professional boundaries.

7. **First, do your own job well, then ask for more.** Do not ask for more opportunities before you have demonstrated the success and value of your current work. You want to send a clear message that you can be counted on to do the job that was expected of you, that you

can handle it, and that you can do more in addition to your currently role, not instead of it.

See also:

Chapter 2: Tools That Build Self-Awareness
Chapter 12: How To Increase Your Visibility Through Strategic Communication
Chapter 14: What To Do When You Make A Mistake

Chapter 11.
How to communicate to build strong, healthy teams

If you can serve as a team lead, this chapter is for you. Building a strong, healthy team will help you weather political storms. Great teams can help avoid gossip and drama, which makes it more difficult for other people to mess with them! Create the kind of team no one can mess with by using some of these suggestions.

1. **Role model communication.** In all cases, demonstrate professional, healthy, supportive communication. Think about what it looks like to show trust in, respect for, and civility toward all team members. Ask for help and feedback and then respond with appreciation and willingness to change. Set expectations and call out problematic behavior that doesn't support those team values. Speak up about concerns with kindness and compassion and support others who do the same. Make it easy for the team to be open and honest with each other. These efforts will send the message that you expect everyone to treat each other with respect, which will curtail unhealthy office politics.

2. **Catch and address problems quickly.** Any concerning communication problem or conflict that arises should be identified and addressed as soon as possible. Unhealthy communication patterns are hard to break once they've been allowed to fester and lead to all kinds of political drama. If you feel there is a lack of awareness and no ill-intent, aim to address these in one-on-one conversations instead of publicly. However, some harmful communication may need to be addressed publicly (see *Section 2: Reactive Strategies: When things go south*), like this: "I've noticed a strange communication pattern between you and Diane recently that I'm trying to understand better. It seems that when she speaks, you find yourself interrupting a lot, which I don't notice you doing with other people. Have you noticed the same thing?" [Regardless of response, you can follow up with:] "I value Diane's perspective as

I value everyone's. I don't want the wrong message to be sent to others that her perspective is less valued or that she deserves to be interrupted. Let's watch this more closely this coming week and see if we can catch it and nip it in the bud. Is there a way I can help you do this?"

3. **Establish clear norms and expectations.** Engage your team in developing clear norms and rules of engagement and how to hold each other accountable for meeting them. Examples include arriving at meetings on time, giving everyone a turn to speak, not interrupting, and participating actively. This helps you develop an environment of respect and mutual support.

4. **Engage in team building and team development activities routinely.** Each time there is a change on the team (e.g., new team member), as well as a few times a year, take time to get to know more about each other as a team and check in on how effective the team is working in meeting goals together. You can also include brief check-ins at the end of certain meetings. Check-ins should include how well you are communicating, how well you come together to approach tasks and address conflict, and the health and safety of your relationships. See below three items for further detail. This again sends a clear message that you expect team members to work well together and that this is an important value, which can curtail negative office politics focused on individual competition and positioning.

5. **Focus on the process of how you communicate and adjust as needed.** How you communicate with your team (the process) is as important as what you communicate (the content). Routinely check in on how you all feel about the frequency, focus, and method for communicating. These types of process-focused communications send a clear message about the value of understanding what works best for everyone instead of just one person. Some questions to consider:

   - Does everyone feel you meet long enough and often enough to address problems effectively?
   - Do you all feel the right information is discussed in meetings?
   - Does the meeting venue (in person, virtually, with or without video, around a table, etc.) meet everyone's needs?

6. **Evaluate the effectiveness of how you approach work and adjust accordingly.** Check in on workflow and decision-making processes. Are there bottlenecks that need to be addressed? Is there a fair distribution of labor that makes sense to the team? Do you each work in sync on certain projects requiring the whole team? Evaluating fairness in the distribution of labor and resources will minimize political maneuvers to hoard resources.

7. **Evaluate the health of your relationships and communications.** A team without respect, civility, and psychological safety cannot get much higher-level work done. How do team members speak with each other? Are there any concerns about feeling undervalued and underappreciated? Look at the behaviors listed in Section 2 to evaluate whether any are occurring on your team that need immediate attention.

8. **There are many more ways to develop hardy teams.** Check out the For Further Reading section for more suggestions.

See also:

Chapter 5: How To Understand Power Through Relationships And Communication Flow
Chapter 20: How To Ask For (Useful) Feedback
Chapter 22: Overt Problematic Behaviors

Chapter 12.
How to increase your visibility through strategic communication

A critical part of proactive communication includes messages beyond your immediate team. Here are a few ways you can elevate the visibility of your work, including tips for how to protect your intellectual contributions from being stolen by others or not credited to you. These tips, as well as those in other proactive communication chapters will also help you develop a presence and tone that will help others treat you professionally and with respect.

1. **Create and share briefings of your work.** For any upcoming meetings, ask your supervisor if they would like you to prepare any briefings, reports, or 1-pagers of positive news and results that align with company goals. In addition, have them ready to go for "quick turn-around" requests.

2. **Offer to attend leadership meetings to answer questions about details of a project only you might know.** Whenever possible, ask to be in the room when any of your work is being presented to important stakeholders. Also invite your staff to be in the room when their own work is being communicated. For example, you could request, "Since the meeting with the VP will be focusing on my team's new database, would it be okay for me to join you so I can answer any specific follow-up questions that may come up about its details?"

3. **Offer to serve on committees on behalf of your boss.** There are times when you might be able to reduce the burden for your boss by joining a committee for which you might have some expertise – a win-win for each of you. Pay attention to when these opportunities might arise and propose the solution, and then make an offer, such as, "You know that committee you mentioned being invited to? Since it's focused on the marketing strategy I've been working on, would it be easier for you if I attended on your behalf, or with you?"

4. **Brand your work.** Whenever possible, add your name, logo, and/or signature to all documents. Ideally when possible, also convert them

to non-editable formats to ensure credit for the work is not lost. Do this for your staff as well as for yourself to help them preserve their intellectual property.

5. **Speak up and share when your projects align with the goals of your organization and leaders.** In meetings with your supervisors and other leaders, share and explain your work in the context of how it helps them achieve organizational goals. For example, you could say, "I've been putting together a list of all the different types of technological solutions we currently have to meet the company's goals of modernizing workflow."

6. **Present at conferences.** Volunteer to present your work at conferences, and practice speaking at larger conferences, moving from regional to national and international levels. When you present, make sure to represent your company well by including their name and logo in your acknowledgements, as well as the names on your team or collaborators. Be inclusive instead of stingy with your acknowledgements – it will serve everyone well and you are more likely to be appreciated for your thoughtfulness.

7. **Learn how to present your work to leaders and stakeholders who do not have your technical expertise.** Leaders and stakeholders have very different interests than those of you and your team. They do not want a long presentation about the technical aspects of your work. Learn what their interests are and how to present the Bottom Line Up Front (BLUF) speaking specifically only to their interests. These are busy people who need to know what will most affect their decision-making. Assume you will be interrupted with questions in the first 3 minutes. Ask yourself "What are the most important high-level points I need to make immediately in the first 2-3 minutes? What is less important for me to share that I would be okay with if we never got to it? Which details are okay to hold back knowing I can always share them if asked?"

8. **Learn how to present using storytelling.** Broad audiences who do not have the background technical expertise that you have need you to present your work in a way they will understand. Learn how to share your work using simply non-jargony concepts building on stories they can relate to (for example, TEDx style talks).

See also:

Chapter 13.
How to maintain visibility as a virtual employee

Virtual (remote) employment has become more common, and we suspect many organizations over time will adopt hybrid models in which employees may spend some time working from home and other time working from the office. In addition, most national and global companies have some employees (usually at one or more headquarters) who work together in person and some spread out throughout the country or world working virtually or in distinct teams that may not always see each other in person. This adds to the layers of politics one must track and manage. Here are a few tips we have seen work well.

1. **Try to travel to the main (headquarters) office routinely.** The main office is where many of the top leaders convene. Try to create a schedule in which you can get in-person time with them (or at least with your most immediate supervisors). This could be once a month if feasible or once a quarter if travel is more difficult. Coordinate with others from the office who may also be traveling for an in-person visit.

2. **If there is a critical conversation to be had but that does not require immediate response, try to save it up for the in-person meeting.** This can include performance discussions, career conversations, a politically sticky situation, or anything related to building trust around sensitive topics. If it's not possible in person, choose to have those conversations over video as the next best thing, and phone as the third best. Avoid having those conversations by email (an email is asynchronous, can be shared with others, and is missing a lot of context, which can lead to more communication problems).

3. **Prepare thoughtfully before every in-person visit about how you can meet new people, develop new relationships with important stakeholders, and help others get to know your personality and your work.** Think also about connecting with anyone with whom you have had a more difficult time connecting with virtually. Set up meetings or dinners with people you might want to develop and

maintain a critical strong relationship with (supervisors, direct reports, important peers and leaders).

4. **Join virtual meetings a few minutes early and stay a few minutes after when possible.** Like in-person situations, this is often a time when you can quickly make better connections with people in the office. You can self-disclose things to help people get to know you and encourage them to share about themselves as well.

5. **Set up individual and group "connect" meetings to intentionally connect with people in the office informally.** This helps you maintain good relationships outside of formal meetings.

6. **If you suspect any miscommunication, set up a meeting to immediately evaluate whether there is a problem that you need to correct.** One of our colleagues shared this story: "In the first few weeks of starting, I was eager to contribute in some way, and I sent an email to someone who worked closely with my team but was on a different team and offered to brainstorm some ideas about an initiative we were working on. The next thing I knew, my boss reached out asking what I had sent to this new colleague, concerned that I was stepping on toes and invading her team's turf. It took a little smoothing over through several 1:1 meetings with the person to restore the relationship. It wasn't as easy as just walking over to the office and clearing things up. I needed to be much more active in setting these meetings up."

7. **When possible, set up specific meetings to review your performance (and the performance of others if you supervise)** so you can get more immediate and regular feedback about any areas that need to be addressed/improved. Ideally you would have briefer check-ins once a month and longer team retreats a few times a year for this purpose.

8. **Be tactful with privacy.** Virtual environments give us insight into others' personal spaces. You may get to see someone's bedroom, pets, kids, or art that you wouldn't normally see. Stay professional. "Cute dog!" is always okay, but otherwise stay away from comments unless you know they will be received well. Similarly, don't record a meeting or take/post screenshots without permission.

9. **Be patient.** This goes for people's pets and kids wandering on screen during meetings, technical problems, "Can you hear me

now?", "You're on mute!" and everything else. Pandemic-style virtual meetings won't be forever, technology will continue to improve, and everyone is doing their best.

See also:

Chapter 14.
What to do when you make a mistake

When you are not able to achieve an outcome, or when there is a misstep that creates an embarrassing or unexpected problem, do not sweep it under the rug or avoid dealing with it. How you choose to address it will make all the difference in how people evaluate your ability to lead and be trusted. Here are some tips for quickly and successfully addressing a mistake.

1. **First talk with people not directly affected by the situation.** In most situations when we make mistakes, we feel so guilty or nervous about the negative consequences that we try to fix them right away, without thinking it through. However, be careful not to jump too quickly – it might create more unintended problems. Instead, first consider talking it out with someone outside of and not affected by the situation. This can include friends, family members, coaches, therapists, mentors, and supervisors.

2. **Do not ask the people directly affected by your mistake to also help you work through your emotions around the error.** When you ask people who were directly affected by your error to also help you manage your guilt, embarrassment, anger, or other emotional reactions, you add a second problem to the first one by placing a burden on them. This is especially a problem for people who are in positions of less power than you (e.g., supervisees, those in lower status positions).

3. **Consider this an opportunity to learn and grow.** All mistakes are an opportunity to learn and improve. Take the time to write down your lessons learned during and after the situation is resolved.

4. **Consider this a hidden opportunity to demonstrate your leadership in sticky situations.** When handled well, a mistake that is addressed well can send the message to others that you can respond to crises maturely and thoughtfully.

5. **Take responsibility for your part.** In most cases, a mistake involves more than one person or one person interacting with a problem in a system. The important thing is to identify and address both what

was out of your control and what was in your control. For whatever was in your control, take responsibility. Consider also communicating a public apology, when possible and appropriate. If there are additional parts of the situation that were outside your control, think carefully about how you can address them. Your ability to identify ways to improve interactions or a kink in the system will further demonstrate leadership if you own up to your part.

6. **Offer a powerful, meaningful, and authentic apology.** A true leader uses the following elements when apologizing:
   a. Go beyond what you intended. Include an acknowledgment of any potentially harmful impact, regardless of your intent.
   b. Describe a specific plan and timeline to improve or correct the mistake.
   c. Request feedback for how to improve or fix the situation or "feedforward" to help you support the effectiveness of your solution (See Chapters 19-21 on giving and receiving feedback).

7. **Follow up fully on whatever plan you offer and feedback you request from others.** Report on the progress and outcome of your attempts to improve or correct the situation as promised. Making, and then keeping, your promise will engender respect and trust in you as a leader.

8. **Use your mistakes to help staff learn and grow.** When you can, share your mistakes with staff and use them as a learning opportunity. Help them understand the context and ask them to walk through the dilemma with you. While not always fun for the ego, this can be a powerful learning opportunity for your staff. Remember to help your staff understand the value of mistakes as an opportunity to learn how to operate differently or take a different approach. Help them embrace and not fear sharing their mistakes.

See also:

Chapter 11: How To Communicate Credibility And Trust
Chapter 20: How To Ask For (Useful) Feedback
Chapter 21: How To Gracefully Accept Feedback And Apply It Effectively

D. Negotiating

There are many books written about negotiating. We have added several recommendations in the reference sections within the following chapters as well as at the end of this book. As opposed to "dirty politics" in which each party takes a position and digs in their heels, good negotiating in "honest politics" can in fact lead to more creative, strategic, longer-lasting outcomes by connecting everyone's interests around a specific common goal while also preserving important relationships. The following chapters describe how to engage in these types of proactive negotiations as well as when to recognize problems and walk away or choose a tougher tactic.

Chapter 15.
The goals of negotiating

The main goal of a proactive and effective negotiation is to help move people out of entrenched ideas and positions. Here are a few ways to do this; at the end of the book, we offer some great resources to dive deeper.

1. **Recognize when you are in a negotiation situation.** Sometimes we don't even notice we have been offered an opportunity to negotiate! Some examples of how to look for these opportunities include:
   a. You are invited to join a meeting in which they want to "talk more about the [idea/suggestion/recommendation/ request]";
   b. You have been offered a new job, role, title, or other opportunity with greater responsibility; or
   c. Someone disagrees with a path you recommend taking for a project.
   In each of these examples, the opportunity has been presented for further conversation to explore whether and how it could work to meet the needs of two or more people. Negotiation is simply engaging in that "whether and how" exploration.
2. **Don't take it personally.** Everyone has a reason for their perspective and why they want to push an idea forward. If the conversation feels tense, use mantras like these to remind yourself: "It's just business" and "My goal is simply to understand the other person's perspective and needs. I don't have to have an immediate solution to our differences."
3. **Approach only if you are committed to finding a mutually acceptable solution.** If you already have your mind set about what you feel is the best solution and aren't open to the potential that this might change, you are not able to negotiate well. You are instead simply putting yourself in a position to argue. Instead allow yourself the opportunity to listen with an open mind and learn the other person's perspective. This will help you refine your goals and co-create better solutions. Keeping an open mind is also a needed and

desired skill for anyone seeking to advance their career to the highest level of an organization as it creates more opportunities for new, better, or more creative ideas to come out.

4. **Listen for opportunities to bring in resources to support mutually beneficial solutions.** Both parties in a negotiation have valuable resources at their disposal that the other may not have. Listen for what those may be and think about the resources you are willing to share.

5. **Consider the possibility that if you are effective, you may end up with more than what you hoped.** Outcomes do not need to be focused on simply addressing one problem. When you are willing and open to work with someone else to address one problem effectively, it often leads to more opportunities to work together and support each other in the future. Go beyond thinking of this as a one-time engagement.

6. **Focus on interests, not positions.** Learn more about the other party's interests and be willing to share your own. What are their goals? What are they hoping to achieve? What are they most concerned about losing or not gaining? It is sometimes easier to solicit this information if you start with your own answers to these questions.

7. **Communicate an interest in meeting organizational needs/goals not just personal needs/goals.** Identify and discuss the "big picture" context. When you approach a negotiation situation in which you only talk about the impact on your work or your team, the other party is less likely to connect with, value, or understand the importance of your interests over their own. Put it into a broader context, for example, "You and I both know that if either of us lose this opportunity, it would crush our programs. If we go in together, it could meet both of our goals as well as the organization's priorities."

8. **Find points of mutual understanding, connection, and value.** Once you put the interests of each party within a broader shared context, explore and discuss how you can meet around some of the goals you both have in common or that are complementary.

9. **Offer opportunities to brainstorm multiple ways of addressing mutual goals.** Avoid digging in your heels, which creates entrenched

positions. Most often, the same goals can be addressed by many different solutions. Be open to the possibility that the other party might have a different solution that can work just as well. The goal is to allow each party a way to back out, save face, and above all, preserve the relationship for future positive and productive negotiations. For example, "I know you want to make this proposal happen, but in the way it's currently written, it will essentially eliminate any chance of there being remaining resources for my own proposal. How can we create a combined proposal that could be more mutually beneficial?"

See also:

Chapter 16.
How to prioritize and choose your battles

You don't have to fight every battle or negotiate for all your needs. Being more discerning about what is important to go after will win you more battles in the long run. This important skill will also demonstrate stronger leadership skills. Here are some ways to help you decide when you should try to negotiate and when you may want to pause.

1. **Don't bargain over everything.** Not everything holds the same level of priority. Over-negotiating can lead to diluting the power of negotiation tactics when they are most needed and exhaust others into wanting to avoid future interactions with you. Make it easy to negotiate with you by demonstrating you can pick your battles wisely and with thoughtful discretion.

2. **Decide in advance what your highest-level priorities are in general, as well as in each situation.** This may include resources (e.g., staff, space, parking), funding lines, or access to information (e.g., serving in critical leadership roles or on committees), among other things. For example, you might decide above all else in any situation, you want to make sure you can hold on to having staff support. That means you would be willing to lose other important things if this is maintained. Then, with each situation, consider what the next highest-level priority or goal is for you.

3. **Decide in advance what you view as your negotiables and non-negotiables.** Negotiables are items you have some wiggle room around. Non-negotiables are items you couldn't reasonably adjust, regardless of any tempting offers you may receive. You should only have one or two non-negotiable items. Any more than that gives the sense that you are thinking too rigidly and limiting the opportunity for a successful outcome. Think about what you are ultimately willing to let go of or compromise on as long as those non-negotiables are adequately met. For example, if you are negotiating in the context of a job offer, your interests might include having a great schedule with flexibility, a specific minimum salary, and a location you want to work from. Based on your current

situation, however, the non-negotiable might be the job location if you can't relocate and the negotiable would be a reduced salary or more restricted schedule to avoid relocation.

4. **After at least one preliminary discussion of the factors in consideration, decide what it will take to say "yes" to the deal.** Do not drag out a negotiation process. Make it easy and painless for those engaging in the process with you to know exactly where you stand and what it would take to finalize the deal. Ideally, this means that once you have (quickly) gathered the information you need about the variables at stake, your priorities, and negotiables and non-negotiables, you then lay it all out for the other party to start engaging with you toward a workable solution. Your goals are to (a) make it easy for the other party to understand your needs, (b) identify a path that minimizes excessive ongoing back-and-forth discussions, and (c) have an opportunity to counter-offer, if needed, in a way that could still meet your needs. It could look like this: "Thank you for taking the time to help me understand the big picture and what is available. I think I could enthusiastically say yes to this opportunity if I could have 3,000 square feet of space and funding for one master's level assistant position for the next 3 years. This would make my transition most manageable and set me up for success. How can we make this happen?"

5. **Test the waters.** Push gently until you get pushback to test out what seems to be points of conflict or tension. This is data that can help inform your next steps. Sometimes, people are not ready for certain types of changes that feel more drastic. Consider when you may need to take more time to explore and introduce the idea slowly.

6. **Consider breaking it down into having multiple conversations and smaller goals.** Not every important conversation needs to happen within one sitting. Sometimes it's more effective to agree to having an initial conversation to simply understand each other's goals and call it a "series of discussions". From that point forward you can then identify smaller goals to accomplish over time, try things out, evaluate outcomes, and adjust as needed, like a series of experiments or pilot tests.

7. **Explore your motivation.** Make sure your motivation for negotiating has integrity. Would this negotiation benefit more than just you? Would this address a conflict in which damage or harm is being done? If not, are there more effective ways to get what you want that you haven't yet tried?

8. **Seek guidance.** Sometimes it's hard to see beyond the immediate pressure to negotiate for things we want. Reach out to a trusted colleague, mentor, or coach to get some additional perspectives.

See also:

Chapter 15: The Goals Of Negotiating
Chapter 17: When To Slow Down Or Back Off
Chapter 18: What To Do When They Don't Negotiate Fairly

Chapter 17.
When to slow down or back off

Not all negotiations will work out. In most cases, this is more of a timing or resources issue. In this chapter, we will talk about identifying when you need to pause or let go of a negotiation due to these windows of opportunity or prioritizing concerns. In the next chapter, we will go into situations when the other party is not playing fair or potentially trapping you into a bad situation.

1. **Notice when things are moving faster than there is time to think thoughtfully about the process.** Often these are times when you are up against tight deadlines or it's a high-stakes situation. In these cases, take a step back to decide how important it is to keep pursuing it or to wait until the intensity of the situation has passed.

2. **Observe the tension in the room.** When the other party becomes defensive, angry, or expresses other strong negative emotions and this seems to be escalating, take stock of what they may be reacting to. Sometimes, this might mean that you are taking an entrenched position instead of seeking mutual interests. Slow down and go back to identifying points of connection. If you think this is more about them not playing fair, check out the next chapter for how to manage it.

3. **Identify when there is insufficient information for decision-making.** There will be times when you thought you had collected the information needed to decide, but the negotiating process seems to indicate you need to gather more. Do not continue trying to negotiate when there is not enough useful data to make a thoughtful decision. You would be better off conducting more background work than negotiating toward a poor outcome.

4. **Evaluate when you need to take more time to understand each other.** People from different fields have their own jargon and ways they approach work which can lead to misunderstanding across fields or divisions of labor. Make sure you slow down when you experience multiple misunderstandings and instead go back to

listening and asking enough questions to create mutual understanding.

5. **Accept that sometimes you have a great idea, but terrible timing.** Losing some negotiation discussions doesn't always mean it was a bad idea. It also doesn't mean you have lost your chance forever. You can always return to it in the future when there is better timing. And while you wait for better timing, you can continue to have further exploratory discussions and gather more data to strengthen your case under better conditions.

6. **Recognize when your idea has merit, but the argument was not strong enough to support it.** Sometimes you believe you have come to the table with all your ducks in a row only to realize half-way through that you hadn't done enough homework. That's okay. Consider it useful data. Acknowledge the situation openly and if possible, request feedback to better understand where the gaps in your argument could have been strengthened for a future attempt to negotiate (see also Chapters 19-21 on giving and receiving feedback). Some additional data to gather when pursuing feedback includes whether the funding request was too high for this year's budget; whether there were similar competing projects being pitched at the same time as yours that you didn't know about; and if you can find out more about those other pitches to better position your argument next time.

7. **Know that in many cases there will be more windows of opportunity to negotiate for similar resources.** This may come up in a different unexpected context. Pay attention and be ready with the materials needed to adjust your request or other ways to get your needs met.

8. **Bow out gracefully if the other party has no actual interest in truly negotiating.** There will be times when you think you are entering into a positive negotiation discussion but realize the other side has no interest in your needs. You may feel bullied, threatened, or bulldozed (see *Section 2: Reactive Strategies: When things go south*). In these situations, it best to gracefully bow out of the conversation. The next chapter describes what to do when they don't play fair.

See also:

Chapter 18.
What to do when they don't negotiate fairly

We'd love for people to always play fair and by "rules" to which we've all agreed. But of course, that doesn't always happen. Here's how to understand when that's happening, and some possibilities for how to respond.

1. **What are your assumptions?** This is a good place to start. Often, we have assumptions about what "rules" we are both playing by that may not be accurate. For example, we may assume that people will tell the truth and that they will negotiate in good faith because that is our approach. It's helpful to clarify what your assumptions are – what "rules" you assumed you both were playing by so that you can understand where other people may have different assumptions or approaches.

2. **Understand what their approach is.** If you've reached the point where you think the other person isn't playing fair, you probably have a good idea of what their approach is. Or it may be that you can guess as to some of the "rules" they are playing by. Maybe you assumed this was between the two of you, but they are choosing to bring their staff and your staff into the argument and sow discord that way. That's helpful to know. Suspend judgment in this moment about whether what they're doing is right or wrong – just try to understand.

3. **Identify your goal.** What is it that you'd like to get out of this conversation? It's helpful to consider your ideal goal, which might be something like: "We resolve this problem and come to an agreement on how we interact and work through problems in the future so that we all feel the parameters are fair." Great! You might also want to consider the more realistic goal that you will not likely change this person. Do you want to win this battle? Win the war? Disempower your opponent so they will leave you and your team alone? Get them fired? Just extricate yourself intact? You have options, and it's worthwhile to consider what you can reasonably work toward.

4. **Identify your allies.** Who supports you? Who will back you up in public? Note not everyone who supports you will back you up in public. If you don't have support from some people, like your boss or other key power people, this might limit your options. If you are faced with a situation that requires having allies to back you up, spend time briefing them and exploring potential options to solving the problem first and ask for their support and/or advice for defusing any potential conflicts.

5. **Identify what rules you'd like to play by in this discussion.** It helps to understand what your values are. We've worked with many clients who are willing to fight dirty if they must. Other clients hold fast to their values, even sometimes at great personal and professional cost. Depending on the situation, you may need to find a balance between holding to your values but also fighting for what you believe is a proper approach. Even if you must play more aggressively, don't lose track of the end goal, and remain professional, civil, and respectful.

6. **Sometimes you lose just by going to the table.** This is high-level politics! Sometimes there are times when it's better just to let it go instead of validating the other person by working with them. The fantastic book "Bargaining with the Devil" discusses these situations. See the "For Further Reading" section.

7. **Consider consequences of different approaches.** It's nearly impossible to rise to a high level in any organization without having at least some people who don't like you. Consider if this is the issue over which you'd like to turn someone into an enemy. Consider the impact of your actions on your reputation, how you are trusted by your staff and others, whether this creates an enemy, how your actions might affect other aspects of your work. Maintaining functional and mutually respectful relationships, even with someone who may not like you or whom you don't like, can mitigate many conflicts. This is an important emotional intelligence characteristic needed in leadership roles as well.

8. **Think strategically, not emotionally.** Yes, you could be angry, irritated, or hurt by the other person choosing to play by different rules. You could think they are a terrible person. That's not important right now. What's important is that you consider your next actions strategically so that you can operate to the benefit of

your team and your goals. Try to let the anger or frustration pass and plan a more strategic response. Taking action when your head is clearer will help you maintain more control over your options.

9. **If you do go to the table, determine whether you want to discuss content, process, or both.** Content will be the nature of what is happening; for example, which team is responsible for doing the thing. Process is getting into the details of how you negotiate and work through problems, which could involve some reference to them not playing fair. First figure out what you want. Many times, just addressing content will work and you can be aware that this person doesn't play fair and work around them as much as possible.

10. **If you want to address the process, consider what you want to get out of the conversation.** Getting the other person to change substantially is not likely. You can merely state your request: "I understand this has been a tough situation. I really encourage you to come to me directly in the future so we can resolve problems faster and easier." You could also be more assertive: "I understand this is a tough situation, but involving my staff is not appropriate. Please work with me directly." You could also be aggressive: "I am aware you tried to involve our staff in this issue that would be better addressed between you and me. Don't do that again." Note that aggressive still does not mean threatening or bullying. It often works to start with a neutral and diplomatic approach and escalate only if needed.

11. **Evaluate your approach.** How did it work? And what would you do differently? Use every experience as an opportunity to learn. Don't be afraid to experience difficult situations or conversations - there is always an opportunity to learn. Some people prefer to avoid negotiating because they fear it will lead to or be experienced as an unnecessary conflict. But sometimes it can't be avoided and sometimes that conversation is the most important thing that needs to happen to move forward with any future steps. At the very least it will give you more data.

12. **Recognize when it's time to let go.** A colleague of ours worked with a client who took a new role within her organization only to learn afterward that she was not told about the true challenges that she'd be faced with, even after engaging in several rounds of negotiation

and exploration to make sure it was all a good fit. She ultimately had to decide whether to stick it out or accept this as a loss. To preserve her reputation and wellness long-term, she ultimately decided to leave her role. See Chapters 39-42 about knowing when to move on for more about how to make these difficult decisions.

See also:

Chapter 1: How To Develop Your Personal Leadership
Chapter 8: How To Build Alliances And Allies Through Strategic Networking
Chapter 15: The Goals Of Negotiating

E. Giving and Receiving Feedback

A lot of the problems that we struggle with related to organizational politics are related to our difficulty giving and receiving feedback. Without feedback, problems go unaddressed and continue to fester, serving as embers waiting to fuel conflict. The next few chapters provide recommendations for ensuring you have done your due diligence surveying and clarifying the root of potential conflict using constructive approaches.

Chapter 19.
How to give effective feedback

Giving feedback is one of the most common sources of difficulties for many of us because of the bad experiences we have had when it goes wrong. Below are some tips for how to make it easier and successful.

1. **If you are in a new job or role, first seek to understand.** When you are in a new context, working with new people, take some time to gather a strong understanding of these new things before giving your opinion about how things need to change. You may still be right, but it is not received as well when you are new because people will believe you are making erroneous assumptions without having sufficient background. Instead, actively ask thoughtful questions to understand the lay of the land and help others see what may not be so clear or obvious to fresh eyes. (See also Chapter 4 on gaining a broader perspective of your organization's history).

2. **If unsolicited, evaluate purpose and timing.** When you feel compelled to provide feedback in the absence of being asked for it, first reflect on what you would like to achieve by offering the feedback and whether the timing is appropriate. For example, if a conflict has turned into a heated argument, a cool-down period would be more helpful than trying to engage in thoughtful dialog. Asking permission to provide feedback will help lower defenses. For example, saying "Would you like to hear my thoughts?", "Can I offer some advice?", or "I'm having a reaction to that – can I share some feedback?"

3. **Do not procrastinate too long or avoid the conflict.** While taking some time to clarify your purpose and determine good timing are important, taking too much time or avoiding the conflict altogether will make the problem worse. Once you avoid addressing a problem several times, it becomes harder to address and a terrible cycle to try to correct.

4. **Make it a routine part of your communication.** Especially if you are in a leadership role, do not wait until the end-of-year performance review to provide feedback. If you do, it will come as a surprise and

91

employees will be disappointed that they had not been given a chance to improve sooner. Instead, make it a routine part of all meetings and let them know about your intention. For example, you could say, "I want to make sure you are never surprised at the end of the year when we review your performance rating. Whenever we meet, I will do my best to carve out time to provide you with feedback on your work performance and how I can support you to reach your goals."

5. **Do not save up feedback – You are not a bank.** It is very confusing, overwhelming, and frustrating to receive a laundry list of critical feedback all at once. A best practice is to provide feedback as soon after an event occurred as possible and only about that event. Over time, if that one problem becomes a habit, it can be discussed in that context, of course. Look for windows of opportunity in which it can be a natural part of the conversation. For example, people often give a window of opportunity when they share their own perception of their work. In that moment, you can respond with feedback such as, "Oh, yes, I recall reacting to that because it didn't sound like the message came across as you may have intended it to...." Also consider how you might offer future-oriented actionable "feedforward" advice when possible. For example, instead of saying, "That presentation you gave could have used some more work!", offer to help them prepare for a future presentation, such as "How are you planning to prepare for this upcoming meeting? What would you do differently from the last presentation? Can I offer some suggestions for the next one?" (See more ideas about using "feedforward" in Chapter 20).

6. **Be as clear and specific as possible.** The words "good job" should never be uttered. It provides no information on why it was a good job, what elements you valued, or how to continue doing a good job in the future in your eyes. Instead, provide examples of what you felt went well, such as, "I really appreciated how you not only put the budget together so quickly, but also included an itemized section for me to better see where the numbers came from and what I might want to adjust when we need new resources." This increases their understanding of what specifically you value so they can reproduce the results you value.

7. **Share positive feedback in public and negative feedback in private.** In most circumstances, make it a habit to praise others publicly and save the concerns for private discussions. Importantly, you want to avoid shaming, embarrassing, or blaming individuals and instead spend time first getting information from them about contributing factors that you may not be aware of and problem-solving to improve in the future. The one main exception to this is when someone makes hostile and harmful comments or actions in public, in which case a public admonishment helps those who are the target of that behavior (see Section 2 for more on how to address these problematic behaviors).

8. **Use "I" statements, facts, and the impact.** Avoid assuming you know what someone else intended, how they feel, or what others think about the same situation. Offer the facts from your perspective and the impact it had. If it is harmful, make sure to be specific and name the behavior. Below are some examples of different models:

   a. *Situation-Behavior-Impact (SBI) model:* "At the meeting we just had [Situation], I noticed Mary share her project and then you interrupted several times to share about your project and expressed it had better outcomes [Behavior, just facts]. This may not have been your intention, but it came off as undermining, invalidating, and dismissive of her work [Impact]. Now, I don't know whether she took it that way, but I was very concerned. Did you notice this? What was your intention? What can you do differently next time?" One could also add constructive feedback at the end of this model as a suggestion for what to do differently in the future.

   b. *Coaching model:* "I have some thoughts on your presentation, but before I share my own, I'd love to hear how you felt about it? What worked well? [listen] What didn't work as well for you? [listen] What would you want to do differently next time? [listen, then add to what was said.]

   c. *Strengths-based:* "Gary, what I appreciate about your work style is that you are really detail-oriented. I always know that the products I will receive from you will be in excellent shape. You gave me a perfect product, but at the expensive of multiple

93

deadline extensions, which pushed our timeline out considerably. How can I help you achieve a better balance between ensuring a great product, but one is 'good enough' to make it on time?"

9. **Be careful of the "compliment sandwich."** The compliment ("crap") sandwich is when you put critical feedback in between two positive pieces of feedback. These days people can see right through it – and they ignore everything you say before the word "…but." It rarely feels sincere and can come off as avoidant. A more elegant way to use this technique is to use the strengths-based approach above.

See also:

Chapter 11: How To Communicate To Build Strong, Healthy Teams
Chapter 22: Overt Problematic Behaviors
Chapter 34: How To Address Treatment That Appears To Be Unfair Or Inequitable

Chapter 20.
How to ask for (useful) feedback

Asking for feedback addresses two goals at once: (1) becoming a more effective leader and (2) developing champions who can support your efforts. The latter goal is how we develop our political savvy. Here are the opportunities that lay before you to seek insight into how you are doing.

1. **Informally ask trusted peers and superiors about how you are doing.** Seek a trusted colleague, mentor or supervisor and ask for their perspective after a presentation you weren't confident about, an email you aren't sure about sending, a negative response you received from someone about how you communicated, or other new experiences. Building a trusted circle where you can go check in on yourself and your improved areas, is key to your development and career advancement as well.

2. **Try to get specific about what kind of feedback you are requesting.** Instead of asking, "How do you think that went?" or "How would you change this?" ask something like, "The message I am trying to convey is ____. Do you think I achieved that? If not, what would you recommend I could change to better convey that message?"

3. **Engage in a 360-degree feedback.** This is a formal process in which you request your boss, superiors, peers, and direct reports to complete an assessment of your competency as a leader and provide feedback for where there is room to grow. Sometimes your company may offer this opportunity, but if it is not available, or if they limit it to only the top leaders within the company, it may still be worth considering paying an external coach/consultant to administer one. Typically, the coach/consultant will administer it, provide you with the results and feedback, and offer to also develop a learning development plan and executive coaching sessions if you are interested in working with them to develop certain skills.

4. **Engage in and prepare thoughtfully for performance reviews with your supervisor.** Send them a self-assessment of your progress, challenges, and goals in advance of the meeting. Challenges you

identify should be tied to your career goals (and ideally also company goals). They should not be a list of complaints without intent to solve them or used as reasons for why you can't accomplish your job. Focus the discussion on improving leadership and management skills for your own professional career goals, as well as achieving specific results for your supervisor. Share a realistic plan and any support you might need, such as regular meetings to review progress. In future meetings with your supervisor, share updates about how you are meeting the goals you discussed together as part of your performance plan. Add ways you may also be going above and beyond.

5. **Ask how else you can help your supervisor be successful.** Feedback is not just about how you can improve as an individual. It is also about how you can improve as an employee, and as part of a team, in supporting organizational goals. Achieving that requires you to have insight into what expectations your own supervisor has in their performance plan that you can help them achieve.

6. **Never ask for feedback unless you truly intend to implement it in some way.** There's nothing more aggravating than being asked to take the time to provide someone with detailed feedback and seeing that they did not take it seriously. Asking for feedback requires sincerity, integrity, and personal accountability for following through. If you ask for feedback simply to "look good" as a performative action, you will lose others' trust in your competency and sincerity quickly.

7. **Focus on bigger leadership-related goals by asking more specific questions.** Don't ask, "What did you think of the images I used in that PowerPoint presentation?" Instead say, "My goal was to explain how this particular strategy could be implemented successfully at a great benefit-to-cost ratio. Did you think that came through in the delivery? Is there anything I could have better clarified or improved to make that even more clear?" This positions you as someone who has an eye toward important high-level organizational considerations and that you want to be seen in this way.

8. **Ask for "feedforward".** In addition to asking how you previously performed (hindsight), you can also ask peers and superiors to let you know how you perform with a future intended action. This

changes the dynamic from being evaluated on past performance to creating champions who want to see you succeed. You are also helping yourself become more visible by asking people to follow and help you improve on an intended goal. Here's one way to ask for this: "I am working on speaking up more in meetings and sharing the work that my team is doing. If you see me improving in that area at our next few team meetings, or if you see missed opportunities when I could have done that and didn't, can you let me know?"

See also:

Chapter 7: How To Become Indispensable
Chapter 12: How To Increase Your Visibility Through Strategic Communication
Chapter 21: How To Gracefully Accept Feedback And Apply It Effectively

Chapter 21.
How to gracefully accept feedback and apply it effectively

If you want others to receive and follow up on your feedback, you will need to role model the same ability. Below are ways you can actively seek feedback and use it to become better at your job, which includes building your political savvy.

1. **Don't argue.** Giving someone critical feedback is not easy to do. It also requires trust. Express appreciation for the person's willingness to be open with you. Make it comfortable for them in the moment and easy for them to feel they can offer it to you again in the future without fear of retaliation.

2. **If you don't trust the feedback or disagree, ask for clarification, or offer to think about it.** Use open-ended non-defensive questions to ask for details and examples. Demonstrate curiosity. For example, you could say, "Thanks for that feedback. Can you say more about this item in my performance review? Can you give me a few examples of what this looked like and how it might show up in the future?" Or you can simply say, "Thank you for the feedback. I'll give it some thought." Then truly give it some thought to evaluate whether your disagreement is stemming from defensiveness, not seeing it the same, needs more exploration, or is totally off-base. Be open to the potential that any of these could be possibilities.

3. **Incorporate your own informal internal 360-degree feedback process.** Seek multiple sources of feedback from others you trust. Listen and assess the feedback provided in the context of other assessments and feedback you have received (see Chapters 1-3 on self-awareness). Are there consistent patterns you are noticing that need to be addressed? Does one piece of feedback stand out as inconsistent with other feedback? If so, what could that mean?

4. **Ask for examples for how you can improve the next rating.** Look for whether the feedback is specific and offers a reasonable path or if it's vague with no clear path. If it doesn't provide you with enough guidance, ask, "How do you imagine it could have been adjusted?"

5. **If you find yourself getting defensive, do an internal gut check.** Feeling defensive is completely normal and even expected. As humans, it's normal to protect ourselves from pain, whether that's physical, emotional, or psychological. Most important is that you allow yourself to observe it, acknowledge and accept that it exists, and then decide what you should do about it. Reflect: Could your reaction be related to your personal certain "hot buttons"? Have others had the same experience with this person or is this specific to this situation? See Chapter 2 on self-awareness for more guidance.

6. **If you receive unsolicited or unexpected feedback, ask yourself whether it's coming from a trusted source before deciding whether and how to use it.** If it's coming from someone you have grown to trust, know that they likely have your best interests at heart. If it's coming from a new source or someone you aren't sure you can trust, thank them for the feedback and then check it against those you know and trust.

7. **Involve the feedback-giver in your plans to improve.** This helps engage those who would like to see you succeed and turns them into champions of your success. It also may discourage non-champions from giving you future feedback if they have no interest in being accountable for the feedback they provide. For example, you could say, "Thanks so much for that helpful feedback. I'll try to use that next time. Can I ask you a favor to let me know if you see an improvement the next time you see me deliver the same message? I really value your observations and it will help me know I'm on the right track."

8. **Remember that feedback is part of a life-long learning journey.** Asking for, receiving, and applying feedback is not easy, but it's critical to your personal and professional growth. Take some time to reflect on what you have gained from following up on past constructive feedback to get you to where you are today, and how you can keep capitalizing on those efforts, and improve your feedback process moving forward.

See also:

Chapter 2: Tools That Build Self-Awareness

Section 2:
Reactive Strategies:
When Things Go South

Section 1 of this book focused on proactive strategies that invite dialogue aimed at achieving mutual understanding (i.e., *moving toward* the conflict to seek connection). However, you can implement proactive strategies perfectly and still encounter harmful political behaviors. When this happens, consider a more intensive approach to respond to what is happening. This section is aimed at setting boundaries and consequences when significant harm is being done (i.e., *moving away or against* the source of the conflict). Signs that a reactive strategy is needed include: power grabs that may feel manipulative or look like attempts to hide or control resources from others, increasing hostility from any individual or team, feeling confused about how people are reacting to you, or seeing clear unfairness, bullying, or other poor behavior. In the first part of this section, we will describe in detail how to identify these behaviors. These behaviors are often aligned with the dishonest self- or community-focused politics we discussed in the Introduction of this book. We will then provide guidance for how to respond to these behaviors as a colleague and as a leader. Section 2C of this book will help you decide if it might be time to cut your losses and leave an unhealthy environment.

A: Identifying Problematic Behaviors

We start this section by first describing a variety of harmful behaviors. Harmful behaviors are those that serve the purpose of trying to create a power imbalance so that the initiator maintains control over financial, management, status, or other resources. They are manipulative and may even be emotionally and psychologically abusive. They persist for as long as they are tolerated or enabled by others. Addressing them early, clearly, and directly is important, especially by people in higher power and at higher levels of the organization. Before we can intervene, however, we must be able to identify harmful behaviors when they are occurring to know how to manage them effectively. Harmful behaviors can often be identified by asking, "Does this serve the company, its mission, its staff, and its customers well?" Another signature mark of harmful behaviors is that they lead to some groups of people consistently being excluded and few being included.

Many times, harmful behaviors are initiated and maintained by a small group of people within a department or division. Unfortunately, however, these behaviors can also be contagious and spread to many more people when there isn't strong leadership to squash them. The perpetrator(s) of harmful behaviors may or may not be fully aware of their poor behavior or its impact. For example, fear or insecurity sometimes drive these behaviors. In many cases, a direct approach to calling it out may be an important initial response to bring this kind of behavior to someone's awareness. Note that many behaviors we will describe go together. For example, when someone tries to undermine you or a process, they may use many methods, such as gossiping, upstaging, and dismissing.

Chapter 22:
Overt problematic behaviors

We start with overt behaviors. These are the ones that are more obvious to catch. The next chapter describes covert behaviors that often happen behind closed doors and harder to catch. All types of harmful but may require different tactics to address. Those tactics will be described after these two chapters on overt and covert behaviors.

1. *Undermining* **is when someone gradually lessens your power, status, expertise, success.** People can also undermine a new process or system if they do not want it to work. People don't always know that they are actively trying to undermine you or a process. For example, they might fear a new change but are unsure how to express their concern. Maybe they had negative experiences in the past when their concerns have been dismissed. In these cases, they might demonstrate their fears through more passive-aggressive means, such as undermining. An example is someone who makes persistent comments to coworkers right before a new system is launched, such as "You know I have read that this new way of doing things doesn't actually work as well as people think. I personally don't think it's better and not sure I feel all that confident it will work. I'm not sure we should be working that hard to make this work out since we'll probably have to go back to the old system anyway."

2. *Belittling* **is when someone makes you feel unimportant or less valued.** Someone might belittle just one person or many people in general. Examples include repeatedly correcting or discrediting someone publicly; questioning someone's decisions; giving advice to an expert at their job; ridiculing, teasing, or making fun of someone; or condescending or patronizing behavior. There is an element of superiority involved in belittling someone else, with the perpetrator sending the message that they believe they are better than the target of their behavior.

3. *Invalidating* **is when someone denies, rejects, ignores, or dismisses your thoughts or feelings.** It sends the message that your concerns

or thoughts are not worthy, valid, or acceptable. This sounds like, "It could be worse, at least..." or "You shouldn't feel that way – you're lucky to even have...." Or "Let's not get overly emotional about this. This is just business."

4. *Gaslighting* **is a form of invalidation that is intended to make you doubt what you experienced and wonder whether you're perceiving reality accurately.** Gaslighting could be statements like, "No, it didn't happen that way," or "You must be forgetting the conversation", or "[Rolling eyes] That's so ridiculous, you're making no sense."

5. *Dismissiveness* **is sending the message that your concerns have no merit or are not worth spending time on.** Think of it like when a judge dismisses a case when it does not have enough evidence to be worth the time for a full hearing. Sometimes dismissiveness can come in the form of nonverbal behaviors like eye rolls or a hand waving away an idea. Other times it might come in the form of passive actions like not taking a meeting with you or only agreeing to set up a very brief meeting to hear your idea (because there is no true interest in hearing your idea). More active actions include quickly rejecting your ideas before giving you sufficient time to share them, with the message being that your ideas are not worth the time. (Note that this is different than when busy leaders who are interested but simply need you to cut to the chase quickly for them to understand your message.)

6. *Gossiping* **is when people share secret or personal information about someone who is not in the room, and often in a sensational and negative manner.** Gossip is often judgmental and puts the subject of the discussion in a negative light. Sometimes gossiping is an attempt to demonstrate having power through access to insider knowledge ("Look what I know that you don't!"). Other times they say they are sharing "to vent" frustrations, but they never actually ask for help to address the problem. Sometimes, they are shared under the guise of being "helpful" or "on your side" such as when someone says, "A lot of people are feeling this way and I'm just the only one willing to be honest with you about it." Either way, gossip conveys a lack of regard for someone's privacy or personal information. Like many of these behaviors, it leads to an erosion of

trust and increases divisiveness among employees. If you are not sure whether to consider it gossip, ask yourself, "How would the subject of this discussion feel if this conversation was recorded and shared with her later? Would she feel pleased? Glad the person was asking for advice on how to handle a problem? Or would she feel betrayed?"

7. *Bad-mouthing* **is like gossip but with a specific intention to slander someone's reputation.** Bad-mouthing is spiteful and often comes from feelings of anger toward someone. This might include blaming someone for the failures of a team project or describing a boss as being incompetent, all within the context of a "secret" discussion in which the subject of the discussion is not present. Both gossiping and bad-mouthing are harmful actions that, when discovered, will forever damage someone's professional optics and label them as someone known for their lack of trustworthiness. Be careful if people like this try to get in your good graces – you may be seen as someone who supports their behavior, or they may take advantage of you. You can be sure they will eventually bad-mouth you.

8. *Upstaging* **is when you try to overshadow or divert attention from someone else to yourself.** Upstaging sends the message that you believe you have more important things to share than the person you just upstaged. In meetings, it often comes in the form of interrupting someone else to demonstrate your superior knowledge. There is an element of competition involved in upstaging in which instead of showing up or communicating as a team, one team member has a need to outshine and outperform others. Observe your own behaviors to make sure you aren't inadvertently doing the upstaging. For example, excitedly interrupting to share your own accomplishments while someone currently has the floor might be seen by others as upstaging.

9. *Bulldozing* **and** *railroading* **are both pushy, overbearing, controlling behaviors that can also involve bullying.** Bulldozing is when you push someone to do something they don't want to do or when you dominate a conversation or relationship. Railroading is when you force a decision to be made quickly or unfairly before someone has enough time to think about it clearly. In work settings, it can often

109

involve dismissive, invalidating, and belittling behavior (see above) combined with more direct and aggressive efforts such as threats or insults. Here's an example of what this sounds like: "This is ridiculous, Sonja. How could it take you this long to make a simple decision? Just check the box and move on already. There's honestly nothing left to think about. Why is this so hard for you to complete? Let's move this along already!"

See also:

Chapter 23: Covert Problematic Behaviors
Chapter 29: How To Respond To Colleague Gossip And Bad Mouthing
Chapter 32: How To Manage The Personal Toll Of Unhealthy Workplace Behaviors

Chapter 23.
Covert problematic behaviors

The following behaviors often use many elements of the overt behaviors described in Chapter 22, but they are harder to catch because they happen in secrecy or through hidden agendas.

1. *Backroom deals* **are negotiations done in secrecy without all the stakeholders present or knowing about it.** You don't find out they happened until after the deal is complete. As a result, they often are experienced by others as being dishonest, even when the intention is simply to get work done faster with fewer people. In addition, they usually include a "quid pro quo" (I do this for you if you do that for me) element that serves the interests of the participants, which again are often experienced as self-serving rather than company-serving.

2. *Backstabbing* **is when someone who appears to be a trusted friend or colleague betrays the relationship.** The betrayal often involves revealing your personal information to others or aiming to take a position or relationship of value away from you in a deceitful way, without you knowing (sometimes not revealed until you discover it by accident). It can include behaviors such as gossiping or bad-mouthing (see Chapter 29). It is a secretive play for power while maintaining the outward appearance of collegiality. Backstabbing could occur in situations in which one peer's career begins to progress faster than another's, creating envy and frustration. From there to betrayal is a thin line. Backstabbing can co-occur with hidden agendas (see below) when someone seeks greater visibility, access to restricted information, or opportunities of promotion, and they take actions behind the scenes to undermine the relationship to gain that access.

3. *Triangulation*, **sometimes called splitting, is when a third person is used in a relationship to manipulate a situation or to passively address a problem with one person through someone else.** Playing one person against another and dividing people to conquer are examples of triangulation. Triangulation can be used in other

harmful behaviors like backstabbing and undermining. One clear sign that it may be happening is if you find yourself having confusing communication problems or conflicts with someone with whom you previously had a good trusting relationship, especially after a new colleague is introduced into the relationship. Another form of triangulation is when someone pulls you into a situation hoping you will fix their problem for them. You just end up in the middle.

4. A *hidden agenda* **is when someone appears to be on board with a plan but secretly has other plans they are trying to achieve.** Hidden agendas are extremely common in work situations involving highly ambitious people and when negotiation is needed. Sometimes it's just in the service of self-protection, like when someone is worried their work will be stolen. Good negotiations and strong communication and relationship building can often uncover those hidden agendas to best meet everyone's needs. Organizations that foster an environment in which everyone is out for themselves and teamwork is less valued than individual achievements are more likely to have employees with hidden agendas. Hidden agendas can often be spotted when you experience people saying one thing but then doing another or agreeing often in meetings but then not following through or even undermining or sabotaging the situation.

5. *Scapegoating* **is blaming, accusing, and singling out someone else for your problems or blaming a small group of people for larger systemic problems.** The purpose is to deflect personal responsibility, explain away failure, and maintain a positive self-image. This behavior is not always within one's awareness – sometimes it's a form of psychological denial to manage feelings of failure and inadequacy. Organizations that do not value speaking up about problems, evaluating problems, improving processes, and learning from mistakes, or ones in which there are harsh punishments for mistakes, are more likely to breed behaviors that involve scapegoating.

6. *Sabotaging* **happens with someone deliberately destroys or damages relationships, projects, or systems to gain an upper hand.** Examples of sabotage include removing support or influence at a critical time for a successful outcome to happen or creating extra hoops for you

to jump through. Sabotage can also involve undermining, backstabbing, gossiping and other similar behaviors already discussed. Some examples include: (a) pumping you for information only to later take credit for the work; (b) talking negatively about you behind your back so your success is marred by a bad reputation, and (c) purposefully excluding you from important decisions that directly affect your success.

7. *Passive-aggressive behaviors* **are indirectly aggressive through actions such as stubbornness, resistance, sabotaging, or inaction.** In more active forms, passive-aggressive behaviors are seen when someone enthusiastically agrees with you in public but then seems to have no intention of following up or supporting the plan. Or when someone seems to complain often but never has interest in engaging in problem-solving. In more subtle forms, it can look like procrastination, avoiding conflict, or using sarcasm or backhanded compliments. The purpose is often to avoid (a) engaging in direct communication about concerns or (b) expressing underlying anger for fear that these types of conversations will be painful or dangerous.

8. *Blocking* **is a power move by supervisors to deny opportunities and is related to sabotaging.** Sometimes blocking can be an unconscious act to keep talented people from leaving. Other times blocking is an act of control or desire to keep opportunities for oneself. It may involve actively not providing approval when requested or more surreptitiously keeping the information guarded.

See also:

Chapter 22: Overt Problematic Behaviors
Chapter 28: How To Respond To Backstabbing, Undermining, And Sabotaging
Chapter 30: How To Respond To Hidden Agendas

Chapter 24.
More problematic behaviors

The following behaviors are often more likely to be systemic and organization-wide. Sometimes these behaviors touch on legal and Human Resource (HR) concerns that might require official investigation through various employee protection policies. There are many resources on each of these topics. We have shared some here as well as at the end of this book in the Further Reading section. We recommend spending as much time as you can learning more about each of these topics.

1. *Microaggressions* **are indirect and subtle messages (whether verbal or non-verbal) of biased and prejudiced attitudes toward someone from a culturally marginalized group.** They are slights, jabs, and stings, sometimes described as "death by a thousand paper cuts." The perpetrator often does not realize when they have committed a microaggression toward someone else, will often deny or become defensive when it's pointed out, and may even believe they were delivering a nice compliment. From the target of the behavior, however, these actions are insulting, derogatory, and hurtful that are perpetrated frequently and casually by many different people across contexts (at work, grocery store, on TV, on social media, etc.). Examples include (a) consistently calling female professors by their first names and male professors by "Dr. [Last Name]"; (b) consistently asking women or people of color to take notes or get coffee (while never asking the same of white or male colleagues); and (c) making comments to a person of color such as "You are so articulate!" - a message of bias that conveys surprise that a person of color would have an unexpectedly strong verbal aptitude (see Sue et al., 2007 in the For Further Reading section).

2. *Racism, sexism, homophobia, ableism, agism and other -isms* **are discriminatory practices and prejudicial attitudes based on the belief that certain people who are part of traditionally marginalized, underrepresented, or oppressed groups (e.g., Black people, women, people from the LGBT community, older people)**

are inferior. In the workplace, it often comes in the form of excluding a group from access to information, resources, power, or opportunity, while including the dominant group. They are more the active and overt forms of aggression as compared to microaggressions.

3. *Implicit (or unconscious) bias* happens when the offender doesn't realize that they are operating with preferences for one individual or group of people while excluding another group or individual. This goes beyond whether someone is a friend or not a friend and includes unconscious decisions about the worth of people. We all have implicit biases. Wondering where you stand with your level of implicit bias? Take the Harvard Implicit Bias Test: https://implicit.harvard.edu/implicit/education.html

4. *Bullying* is when someone uses their power to coerce, harm, control, intimidate, dominate, or abuse others. Bullying is usually a repeated and ongoing behavior. Power differences may be related to physical differences, age differences, or even having access to secret information. We think about bullying when it's physical but at work, it usually comes in verbal (e.g., teasing, insulting, threatening), and social (e.g., gossiping, backstabbing, undermining) forms.

5. *Harassment* is considered employment discrimination that violates Title VII of the Civil Rights Act of 1964, the Age Discrimination in Employment Act of 1967, (ADEA), and the Americans with Disabilities Act of 1990, (ADA). Protected groups in the U.S. include race/ethnicity, religion, sex, pregnancy, national origin, age, and disability. In most workplaces, a case can be made when the discriminatory behavior is toward any of these protected groups, when the behavior continues but is unwanted, and when it affects conditions of continued employment. This is important to know when considering the options we describe in the following chapters.

See also:

Chapter 25: How To Evaluate The Problem To Choose The Right Solution
Chapter 31: How To Respond To Hostile Comments And Behavior

Chapter 38: How To Best Work With Human Resources And Legal Counsel

B: Specific Strategies for Responding to Harmful Behaviors

We will start by sharing general strategies that should be used in most circumstances. Whether they work or not, it is important to try these first to document efforts to reach a resolution at the lowest level before resorting to more intensive and aggressive approaches that might have a greater impact on your job or might require more significant time investment. Consider what might be appropriate in responding when you are the person's peer compared to if you are their supervisor or have other authoritative power. Remember that this is just a start and there are many more skills to learn the more complex and harmful the behavior is.

Chapter 25.
How to evaluate the problem to choose the right solution

Before you do anything, take time to reflect on the situation, evaluate what may be happening (who is contributing to what piece of the problem?), and try to de-escalate the situation if possible.

1. **Pause and take time to reflect on your reaction whenever possible.** The adage "sleep on it" applies here. Sometimes our emotional reactions are strong, overwhelming, and confusing. Taking time to first clarify and make sense of your reaction allows you to take a more intentional and thoughtful approach and can give you a greater sense of control. Developing this also helps you develop your emotional intelligence. (See also Chapters 1-3 on self-awareness).

2. **Evaluate your contribution.** Is there anything you might be doing that is escalating the conflict? Are you avoiding speaking up and letting someone know how the behavior is affecting you and therefore implicitly sending a message that it's okay? Or are you immediately going on the defensive without pausing to reflect whether you may be complicit in the problem? Are you supporting harmful behaviors toward others by laughing at hurtful jokes but then upset when it happens to you? Are you smiling at harmful behavior to manage internal anger you find hard to control? All of these require thoughtful reflection to determine next steps.

3. **Seek consultation.** Get feedback from others when possible. Seek more objective peer consultation to help you step outside of your subjective experience and see additional angles you might be missing.

4. **Aim toward addressing the conflict in a constructive vs destructive way.** Constructive conflict involves surfacing and communicating the concern, clarifying the issues through a collaborative and curious approach, and taking a learning and growth stance. You can tell it's becoming destructive if you experience entrenched positions

(i.e., people digging in their heels), a combative stance, or attempts to create win-lose instead of win-win outcomes.

5. **If you feel put on the spot and feel like you are freezing up, create space for yourself to think by asking clarifying questions.** For example, "Can you give me an example?" or "Can you say more?"

6. **Try to invite additional team input for more perspectives - if it seems appropriate.** Additional team involvement is appropriate if you feel the problem affects the whole team. It's not appropriate when the goal is to force people to take sides or if the behavior is not about the group. For example, some supervisors drag the whole team into a problem because they are avoiding talking directly to an individual about a performance or conduct problem. This is not fair to the team. Consider carefully if, and when, the team needs to be involved.

7. **Avoid being cajoled into letting the inappropriate or harmful behavior go unaddressed.** For example, do not let someone bully you into accepting the behavior. Also do not accept favors, gifts, or other items that might create a further imbalance of power.

8. **Be above the insults.** Stay ruthlessly focused on seeking a resolution through objective means. That does not mean avoid standing up for yourself. But it does mean focusing more heavily on the process and less on the content. The process needs to aim toward constructive vs destructive conflict resolution (see #4 above). The content needs to only focus on stating the simple facts about the concern and potential common interests, while actively avoiding falling into the trap of hurling insults back, becoming defensive at inaccurately portrayed information, or other attempts to sabotage the discussion. (See Chapters 15-18 on negotiating and Chapters 19-21 on giving and receiving feedback for some additional tips).

See also:

Chapter 26.
How to directly address minor harmful behaviors

Sometimes staff or colleagues have behaviors that are annoying and problematic, but not truly awful. These are behaviors like minor gossip, occasionally taking credit for others' work, minor disagreements with others, or being unprofessional in small ways. Generally, it's ideal to address the problem directly and swiftly. If you feel you have enough power and safety to do so, here are some tips for making it effective.

1. **In general, give critical feedback in private and praise in public.** However, if the behavior is egregious enough, it may need to be addressed immediately in public to demonstrate your commitment to addressing problems head-on and send a message that it will not be supported or tolerated.

2. **Scan your own emotions first** and make sure you can address the problem from a position of facts/policy and empathy when possible, in a matter-of-fact way to avoid escalating the situation.

3. **Prepare your talking points before a difficult feedback conversation, aiming to give feedback that is accurate, fair, and actionable.** You could also role-play the situation with someone outside of work. Stop the conversation as needed to brainstorm how you might address different ways in which the feedback recipient might respond.

4. **Feedback should be concise and clear.** "I'm not quite sure what the intention was behind making a comment like that, but it was disrespectful and not consistent with our values. I'm sorry that the team had to hear that. Let's talk further about this in private about how to more productively address the frustration behind that comment." In difficult conversations, make sure to ask the recipient what questions they have, but don't tolerate an argument about who is right or wrong. Ensure they know the expectations for behavior and encourage them to contact you with any questions in the future.

5. **When possible, make a human connection in your feedback about inappropriate behavior.** For example, "I just heard you suggest she should 'go back to your country', which really shocked me – as

someone who grew up in a different country myself, I personally found that very hurtful and offensive. It didn't seem consistent with what I know of you. [Turn to target] Are you okay? Should we talk further about this?" If there is no relationship with the aggressor or it feels unsafe to call them out, then help the person who was the target of the poor behavior leave the situation and determine how to report the incident when in a safe place to do so. If you are the direct supervisor of the person exhibiting this inappropriate behavior, make sure it's addressed immediately through the appropriate feedback and management mechanisms of the company.

6. **When possible, get feedback from others after a difficult interaction so you can learn from the situation.** Make sure to involve the employee who is the target of the inappropriate behavior to help you determine their comfort level in your gathering feedback. Sometimes you need to simply inform them of what you are doing. Other times, you have more leeway to make a collaborative plan. Seek Human Resources guidance in this area. For example, you can say to a trusted colleague, "I just had to correct an employee in a meeting. Can I discuss with you?" Remember that the goal is not to gossip or vent your frustration but rather to learn how you can continue to improve this skill.

7. **Identify ahead of time what you think the best-case scenario is for the difficult feedback.** Sometimes, it might not be possible both to give honest feedback and to not hurt their feelings. Identify what you want to occur because of your conversation and how to get there.

8. **It may be appropriate to ask if something else is going on with the person.** If the person indicates there may be a personal problem outside of work that is affecting their performance, suggest they can talk with the Employee Assistance Program or Human Resources. Indicate they do not need to share details with you (in fact, sometimes people want to share all the details to manipulate you into feeling sorry for them so they can continue to deflect responsibility). Express concern and work with them to address the task at hand.

9. **This is an excellent opportunity to make this a learning experience for your staff and to model appropriate behavior.** Of course, it's not

always possible to discuss these situations publicly. If possible, however, discuss difficult items forthrightly, be compassionate, listen, and move forward.

10. **If possible, remove problematic people from any roles that will create more contagion, especially those in leadership roles.** If these are supervisees, reassign them to other roles to separate them from roles involving access to productive people, sensitive information, and decision-making.

11. **If providing feedback on minor behavioral problems is an area of struggle for you, consider whether the Human Resources office has online training or can provide consultation to assist you with providing feedback.** Also consider reading classic books *Difficult Conversations: How to Discuss What Matters Most* by Douglas Stone, Bruce Patton & Sheila Heen and *Crucial Conversations: Tools for Talking When Stakes Are High* by Al Switzler, Joseph Grenny, and Ron McMillan (listed in the For Further Reading section). You can also identify someone who seems good at providing feedback and ask them how they do it.

See also:

Chapter 19: How To Give Effective Feedback
Chapter 21: How To Gracefully Accept Feedback And Apply It Effectively
Chapter 38: How To Best Work With Human Resources And Legal Counsel

Chapter 27.
How to respond to others persistently taking credit for your work

You worked with a colleague on a project, but they present it as their own and don't acknowledge your contributions. You notice a senior leader took credit for work that was done by someone at a lower level in the organization several months ago. These are examples of "dishonest self-focused" politics at play (see Introduction for more information). It is so frustrating when someone else takes credit for your work! There are several ways to address this issue to make sure it doesn't happen more than once.

1. **For a new project, attempt to clarify who will do what part and how credit will be allocated.** Ensure everyone is clear on the breakdown of roles and responsibilities. Try to work with colleagues who share responsibility and credit, if possible. You can also keep notes about who is doing what for each project. This documentation may come in handy later to refresh your memory if you need it. There are many project management tools out there to do this. One is called roles and responsibility charting and you can find out more here: https://pmicie.org/files/22/PM-Toolkit/85/racirweb31.pdf

2. **When possible, talk to the person who took credit for your work to let them know you saw what they did and that it wasn't cool.** Sometimes this is enough. If it was someone in a higher leadership role, seek out a mentor or supervisor who can help you decide what might be done to address this – in some cases, they can take it up directly through their own relationship channels.

3. **Build relationships with colleagues; they may be less likely to take credit for your work if they have a genuine connection with you.** Consider meeting with colleagues to discuss how credit is allocated and to share your perspective and values around giving credit where it's due. Can you all share credit, or take turns having primary credit across different projects so you all benefit? You can also develop this meeting into an informal peer mentoring group.

4. **Limit how you share sensitive information if you think they might not use it well or might use it against you.** For example, if someone regularly tries to take credit for your work, you might not want to share that you will be out of the office for a death in the family. That is information someone could use to take over part of your project or suggest you're not fully functioning at work.
5. **Consider talking to your boss or the person running the project to clarify what happened and ask for advice regarding how to proceed.**
6. **Observe the environment where you work to identify if this is a common and accepted occurrence or whether it is generally discouraged.** If it is a common and accepted occurrence, consider whether this is the right work environment for you.
7. **Identify which types of projects can be done alone versus which need to be split amongst employees.** Think about which person has the proper expertise for the subject area, so roles and contributions can be defined early.
8. **Adjust your expectations about the kind of relationship you can have with people who take credit for work.** Take steps to ensure fairness and know you might not have the kind of collegial relationship you would like.
9. **If you frequently feel like people are taking advantage of you,** you may want to consider obtaining a coach or therapist who can help you through this challenge so that you can break the patterns and feel better.
10. **In organizations where similar presentations are made by many people, sometimes people end up copying each other's presentations without thought to acknowledging credit.** If you notice this happening, bring this issue up as an organizational concern, with a desire to create a policy that will help all staff (including leaders) be more thoughtful and fair in how acknowledgments for work are recognized.
11. **Never take credit for other people's work.** Remember that if you do not want it done to you, make sure you do not do it to others. Always consider who contributed to the work you are presenting and make sure to acknowledge those contributions publicly.

See also:

Chapter 28.
How to respond to backstabbing, undermining, and sabotaging

Poor behavior happens. That's a polite way to say that sometimes people do terrible things. How do you respond to backstabbing, undermining, sabotage, and backroom deals? Read on…

1. **Sometimes it's useful to assume that the behavior was just a misunderstanding.** If you want to take this approach, you can provide feedback by pointing out the behavior and seeing if/how it is acknowledged. For example, you could say, "I'm not sure you realized this when you did it, but sharing the email I sent only to you with your whole staff to complain about something you disagree with me about undermines me and undermines our trust and relationship. If you disagree with me, I'd like to help address it directly. That will help us maintain a strong, supportive relationship." If it happens a second time, remind the colleague of the previous talk and the link between the two situations as a concerning pattern. Then document the behavior and your response (without emotion and personal bias or assumptions – just the facts). Ideally, the behavior will be addressed at the lowest level possible. However, the documentation will help demonstrate what you have already tried if it needs to be escalated to a higher level or Human Resources.

2. **If people are backstabbing, undermining, or sabotaging, they might not care about maintaining a strong, supportive relationship.** If you think this is the case or you have tried assuming the best, and it didn't work, it's time for alternate approaches. First, understand that their goals or approaches may not be consistent with yours. If you continue to assume they value what you value, you will continue to be blindsided.

3. **Address your emotions.** It's okay to feel hurt, angry, sad, furious, shocked, or anything else. You don't have to act like you don't have feelings! It's also helpful to notice the feelings and set them aside so you can work through what to do next. Vent as you need to (only

with trusted colleagues or friends), then roll up your sleeves and get to work. Keep in mind that venting without a plan of action adds to poor behavior and may be seen as gossip. Read further about how to seek appropriate support.

4. **Identify your allies.** Who supports you? Who will back you up in public? Note not everyone who supports you will back you up in public. If you don't have support from some people, like your boss or other key power people, this might limit your options. Ensure you know who has your back as you consider how to move forward.

5. **Seek consultation and support from a trusted peer, coach, mentor, or supervisor.** Be careful not to use that time to vent or gossip, but rather to seek an additional objective perspective, emotional support, and guidance for problem-solving. You might want to say diplomatically, with a specific and brief example, "I am realizing that I have a colleague who is sabotaging me. For example, they told me outside a meeting they support me, but in the meeting attacked me and my ideas. This has become a pattern with this colleague. I'd like to chat about how to approach it." Then you can follow up with questions like, "What have you done in similar situations?" or "How can I address this in the moment?" or "How can I discuss with them privately?" and "What do you recommend for moving forward?"

6. **Determine whether it's better to work with the person, around the person, or confront them.** People who do these kinds of behaviors are often difficult to work with and unlikely to respond to a diplomatic approach. Often, they seek or wish to hold on to power. They may also be protected in some untouchable way. You need to decide what is most important and why. At times, the answer may be to give them what they want. This shouldn't be your only go-to practice, but there may be more important battles to fight than this one. Other times you can work around them by limiting contact, working to restructure your teams so you don't have as much interaction, corralling supportive colleagues who can neutralize their aggression, relying on a boss or other senior person to intervene the issue, or just ignoring the poor behavior and continuing on your way. Finally, there will be times when standing up to them will be your best and most important approach. For example, if they are undermining you publicly, calling them out on it may help them

realize their impact (if they don't already know), hear that you will not tolerate being mistreated, and help others respect you and perhaps even gain confidence to do the same when they are mistreated.

7. **Consider whether it makes sense to talk with your boss directly.** Your boss is usually one of the best people to talk with first about responding to these situations. Unfortunately, if you are in one of the unfortunate situations in which your boss has not always demonstrated support or sound advice, you may first need to evaluate your boss's potential awareness or involvement in condoning the behavior, and whether he/she may still be open to this discussion. Approach it not as a complaint but as an effort toward problem-solving. If it's about your boss, you could say something like, "I notice that I haven't been included in some critical meetings, and that's limiting my effectiveness. Can we discuss how to resolve this?" Note in this example, it could be that your boss just tells you that you no longer need to go to the meetings. Consider how you'd like to respond to that! If it's about someone else, you could say something like, "Here is what I'm seeing [situation and behavior]. It's affecting my ability to focus and provide an optimal product to you [impact]. Here is what I have already tried... Do you have any other recommendations I can try to address this?" (See also Chapter 19 on how to give effective feedback).

8. **Cultivate your relationships with allies and defend each other.** If you can't remove the person or remove yourself, you can encourage your allies to help you, especially if they also are attacked by this person. For example, you could say something like, "I don't like the way Bob reacted to you in the meeting the other day. I think your point was good and he was rude. I wasn't sure what to say in the moment, but is there a way that would be helpful for me to support you? I notice he sometimes does that in meetings and would love for us to help out each other."

9. **If you notice a pattern of being treated poorly at work, it might be helpful to address with a therapist, coach, or mentor.** Not because being treated poorly means there is something wrong with you, but

133

because any pattern might be helpful for you to understand more fully and to get another perspective and advice for how to manage it.

10. **If the behavior is accompanied by more hostile interactions that make it feel unsafe to address directly, see the "responding to hostile comments and behavior" chapter below.**

See also:

Chapter 29.
How to respond to colleague gossip and bad-mouthing

Gossip is not always bad. Every organization relies on word of mouth to pass information and opportunities along. Good strategic information is invaluable for helping you climb the ladder. Every organization, however, also has a few gossips who seem to revel in negative information about people. These are the people who delight in passing along negative information about other people or stirring up problems. It's important to know the difference between word-of-mouth information and negative gossip.

1. **Do not engage in negative gossip about people, either to listen or to pass along.** When people start to gossip, walk away, or find something else to do – respectfully and professionally when possible. For example, saying things like "Oh, I'm sorry, I have to run to prep for my next meeting." Do not share private information or negative gossip in areas where you are not sure you are alone (e.g., in a bathroom).

2. **It may be that when you are not present, you will be gossiped about.** Keep the amount of information you share to a minimum to reduce what they can share about you. You don't have to spend time with people who gossip – it makes sense to be concerned you'll soon be the target of their negative gossip as well. If you feel you must engage with some office gossip, provide a very general and non-controversial response, such as "huh," and then leave the conversation.

3. **Consider that some people often do know about useful information before others.** Consider carefully if you choose to engage to trade information with them. Be sure you are acting in accordance with your values and sense of integrity and not engaging in anything negative or that you will regret.

4. **Learn how to avoid gossip.** Read the book *No More Team Drama: Ending the Gossip, Cliques, and Other Crap that Damage Workplace*

135

Teams by Joe Mull to get more insight on how to reduce gossip and build relationships (details listed in the For Further Reading section). Yes, this is such an important topic, we are just going to make the recommendation to read an entire book about it! You can also find someone who seems very good at staying out of negative gossip and ask them how they do it. Keep in mind that it's not just about avoiding doing the gossiping, but also avoiding being perceived as part of the group that gossips. Many people do not realize just how much being perceived as supporting "the gossip group" can damage your peer relationships, reputation, and future career opportunities within a company.

5. **Create a mantra you can use when people try to pull you into negative gossip,** such as, "Huh. I don't see it that way" or "I don't feel comfortable talking about people like that when they're not here."

6. **Limit your social media relationship with colleagues who typically engage in negative gossip.** You may want to maximize your social media relationships with people who share useful positive or neutral information.

7. **If you're having a problem at work, talk to someone you trust outside of work for an external opinion.** Don't vent to work colleagues as it is likely to end up being seen as gossip and being shared around with others.

8. **Adjust your expectations about the kind of relationship you can have with overly gossipy colleagues.** Take steps to ensure fairness. Also know you might not have the kind of collegial relationship you would like with those colleagues.

See also:

Chapter 22: Overt Problematic Behaviors
Chapter 25: How To Evaluate The Problem To Choose The Right Solution
Chapter 37: How To Intervene On Behalf Of Others

Chapter 30.
How to respond to hidden agendas

Wouldn't life be grand if everyone said what they meant and meant what they said? Maybe or maybe not, but that is not the world we live in! Look at how to identify and respond to hidden agendas.

1. **Notice consistencies and inconsistencies between what people say and what they do.** Similarly, you can look at the values of the organization and what leaders do, or the stated intentions compared to the actual impact of the behavior. Not all inconsistencies are bad, but it's helpful to get better at noticing. What people do will reveal more about their actual agenda than what they say.

2. **Many of us default to trusting what people say as their truth.** This is healthy because we need to be able to communicate clearly and accurately in a society in which we rely upon each other. That said, many people will say one thing and do another. And what they do is often their actual truth. Notice if you have this default, especially if you're in confusing workplace politics situations.

3. **When you notice inconsistencies, don't automatically call out the person.** Instead, do your homework, stow it away, and track the behavior so you can understand it more. It will be helpful to identify the extent of these inconsistencies within your team or across the organization; for example, some organizations have a culture that leaders are only allowed to say positive things in front of staff, regardless of what is happening. Some organizations say that respect is a critical part of their culture, yet let some people get away with being disrespectful. Be your own detective and try to understand what's going on.

4. **Consider your goal.** At first, your goal is probably to figure out what's going on. As you learn more, you may have goals of confronting the person to get them to change their behavior, urging the organization to be more internally consistent, or stopping poor behavior. Consider that you're unlikely to change an individual's approach or a company's strategy unless you are very senior and

have considerable power (or powerful allies). Depending on the nature of the situation, often it's helpful just to be aware of the multiple agendas and to proceed more thoughtfully.

5. **Identify the right strategy to address the issue.** You have options. It may make sense to speak with others to indirectly ask about the issue, talk with one person privately and directly about the issue, address it publicly in a meeting, or work behind the scenes to make changes. Options also have consequences. Decide if it's worth engaging directly with them. Can you work with them if there is a way to still meet business goals with integrity? Or do you feel it may be better to limit information and decision-making until you evaluate further? You might be able to provide feedback to a person or group by saying, "This is confusing. I am hearing x but seeing y. Can you help me understand?"

6. **Of course, if safety is at risk or crimes are being committed, this dramatically escalates the urgency with which you should address the situation.** For immediate safety issues, you may want to talk with your supervisor, quality assurance, Human Resources, or an inspector general at your organization. For suspicions of criminal behavior, talk to a lawyer that represents you (not the company lawyer). See Chapter 38 for more detail about when and how to seek Human Resources or legal counsel.

7. **Protect your staff.** If you're seeing inconsistencies, your staff probably are too. It's important to confirm their reality while also protecting them from political fallout if it's possible. You could say, for example, "I understand there has been some discussion about what people say and what they do. I'm seeing some discrepancies too, and I want to confirm your perceptions. At the same time, I want to get more information and understand what's going on before acting. I request that you do not discuss amongst yourselves; if you have questions, please bring them directly to me."

See also:

Chapter 19: How To Give Effective Feedback
Chapter 25: How To Evaluate The Problem To Choose The Right Solution

Chapter 38: How To Best Work With Human Resources And Legal Counsel

Chapter 31.
How to respond to hostile comments and behavior

Bullies aren't only for grade school: Some people never grow out of bullying others. Sometimes someone may say they support you in private, but then in public they undermine you by not giving you proper credit, blaming you for problems, or suggesting indirectly that you are not good at your job. You don't have to put up with sexual harassment, microaggressions, overt aggression, bullying, racist, sexist, homophobic or other hostile comments and behavior!

1. **Clarify what is happening:** Does it directly affect your work? Is it about your work? Is it about your personal life (beliefs, appearance, religion, sexual orientation, race, gender, age, disability, or gender presentation)? This could determine the way you need to deal with it. Generally poor behavior related to things like gender, race, disability, age, and religion could be considered unlawful harassment at work, whereas other kinds of poor behavior may not be. In fact, there are laws protecting specific "classes" or groups of people who have traditionally been oppressed, marginalized, or prohibited from equal access. Know your organization's policies and the laws on this.

2. **Document incidents of bullying or undermining, even if it's only in your own note log.** Consider emailing notes to yourself so you have a time/date stamp. Have "receipts" you can go back to.

3. **Know your organization's policies and your rights related to sexual harassment and other unlawful workplace behavior.** In the U.S., repeated unwanted sexual comments, propositions, or touching can be considered sexual harassment and can be against the law. Some hostile behavior is egregious even if committed only once or if it's not sexual in nature. Check your organization's policies for how they address harassment. This policy will outline acceptable and unacceptable behavior and indicate whom to contact if there is a problem. Generally, the process to address sexual harassment is to (a) ask the harasser to stop if it is safe to do so, then (b) report the behavior to the appropriate internal office (Equal Employment

Opportunity Office, Office of Diversity, Equity, and Inclusion) and/or your supervisor with a specific request. If there is no official response or if the response is weak (asking you to stop creating trouble, not taking it seriously), you may want to consider external support measures such as obtaining a lawyer and/or leaving the organization. Also see Chapter 38 on seeking Human Resources or legal counsel for how best to use them as a resource.

4. **Get support from others, including friends or family.** Be cautious discussing the situation too broadly – be thoughtful about who needs to know and who could be helpful to you. If you happen to know a friend who experienced harassment, bullying, or other hostile behavior, you may want to share what is happening to you and ask what they recommend. The usual course of action is often to first report the concern to your direct supervisor, or Human Resources if you feel uncomfortable bringing it to your supervisor. Some companies also have an anonymous hotline set up for reporting concerns like these.

5. **Consider talking with a colleague in the organization about their perspectives on civility and courtesy generally to see if they have self-awareness and would be open to providing feedback.** You could say, "I've noticed that people seem to speak to each other harshly here and that there's a general environment of joking and ribbing. I like to have fun too, but sometimes it seems to go too far. What do you think?"

6. **Observe the environment where you work to identify if hostile behavior is a common and accepted occurrence or whether it is generally discouraged.** If it is a common and accepted occurrence, consider whether this is the right work environment for you.

7. **Have a discussion with your boss about your perceptions of the situation when a bullying or other hostile situation happens.** Identify what you observed and ask for their perspective, such as by saying, "It seemed like this was intentional; can you help me understand what happened?" Most people will respond kindly and attempt to make the situation better. If they don't, that raises a big red flag.

8. **Consider what the person's motive might be--is it personal to them, are they threatened by you, or is this just how they behave?** Their

142

motives do not excuse their poor behavior. Understanding their motives may help you understand how to counter them and protect yourself.

9. **Do not give these people any more information about yourself, your feelings, or your inner life to use against you.** Consider whether it may make sense to limit your public expressions of disappointment or hurt. Sometimes it is better to not give people like this the satisfaction.

10. **Identify colleagues who can stand up for you.** Sometimes even when you can't defend yourself, someone else can defend you, and then you can defend each other.

11. **Adjust your expectations about the kind of relationship you can have with people like this, and the kind of support they can give you.** Take steps to improve the process so you can do your work - but know you might not have the kind of collegial relationship you would like. Remember, it is a reflection on the other person, not on you, if you are bullied, undermined, or harassed.

12. **If your efforts aren't working, consider that this may be an unsustainable situation and you may need to seek employment elsewhere.** If it is possible, consider switching groups or teams in your organization so you are not working with the bully or underminer.

13. **If you have a pattern of being bullied,** you may want to consider talking with a therapist about how to break these patterns.

14. Read *The Asshole Survival Guide: How to Deal with People who Treat you Like Dirt* by **Robert Sutton** (details listed in the For Further Reading section).

See also:

Chapter 24: More Problematic Behaviors
Chapter 38: How To Best Work With Human Resources And Legal Counsel
Chapter 42: How To Assess Your Options, Make A Decision, And Stick To It

Chapter 32.
How to manage the personal toll of unhealthy workplace behaviors

Responding to unhealthy behaviors in the workplace takes a personal toll. You may find yourself disappointed, hurt, angry, and even cynical toward others. Here are some tips for taking care of yourself so you can maintain the fortitude to stay focused, productive, and keep going.

1. **Take care of yourself through mentorship, supervision, coaching, therapy, Human Resources, Employee Assistance Programs, and other professional support as needed.** This can provide you with additional objective perspectives to help you reflect on the experience and process it. Review Chapters 1-3 on self-awareness and Chapter 38 on how to work with Human Resources and legal counsel for the differences between how each of these can help.

2. **Cultivate allies and sponsors at work.** Allies are people who have your back and will support you, advocate for you when appropriate, and even fight for your cause if appropriate. They do not let you wallow for too long in your misery. Instead, they can help you jump into action when needed, and sometimes even jump in with you. When you call someone out for harmful behavior, they are the ones who will amplify the message by verbally supporting it and adding their perspectives to what you said. They help you feel like you are not alone or going crazy. One common example of this is when women in male-dominated organizations agree to speak up when any of the women at a meeting is interrupted or has an idea stolen by a male colleague (a common experience): "Hold on, Mary started speaking and I'd like to hear her finish what she was saying." Or "Yes, great idea, Michael – sounds like what you were originally proposing, right, Angela? Angela, can you share more about that proposal?"

3. **Find your compass and stay aligned.** Remind yourself of your values, goals, and purpose and stay aligned with them. We feel less disconnected, confused, and frustrated when our actions are strongly aligned with our values, goals, and purpose. When that

alignment is not there, we feel a lot more internal turmoil and we start making bad choices to address this misalignment. This is called *cognitive dissonance*. Our efforts to rid ourselves of cognitive dissonance can cause many more problems because we start compromising our values. Instead, the goal is to seek the right kind of discomfort that allows us to become more aligned with our values rather than to compromise them.

4. **Watch for signs of projection as a message to seek help.** Projection is when you take the negative emotions and judgments that you don't want to have about yourself and you put them on someone else to deal with. For example, coming home and immediately snapping at your children for being inept - after a day when you felt completely inept and your confidence was shaken. The more stressed out we get at work, the more likely we are to project it on other people, especially those we care about. This happens because it's safer to take our frustration out on people who have unconditional love for us than to directly address it with people we consider to be unsafe and who do not handle us with care. To avoid losing the very people who care about us, we must seek help when we find ourselves repeatedly projecting our anger and stress on them.

5. **Take care of your physical health.** Exercise and healthy eating are often the first positive habits we give up on when we are under extreme stress. We want to just crawl up under our blankets, eat a large pizza and ice cream, and watch TV for hours rather than do the hard work of exercising and making a healthy meal. But our coping resources get significantly depleted, at a much faster rate, when we give up on ourselves in this way. Ask a buddy (an "accountability partner") to help you stay on track with these important life routines if needed.

6. **Make room for routine but rewarding non-work time.** Engage in hobbies, take walks outside, call friends, take vacations. Make sure every day includes some portion of time that has nothing to do with work. Ideally, this activity should be rewarding, meaningful, and fulfilling in ways that are very different from what your job might offer. This helps you rebalance your focus, remind you what (and

who) is important in your life, and connect with your values and priorities (see #3).

7. **Counter-balance toxic workplaces with positive, healthy relationships.** When dealing with unhealthy behaviors or relationships, it's easy to start feeling cynical - as if the whole world is like this - because those behaviors take up so much of our time to manage. Counterbalance these experiences with inviting, seeking, and connecting with people in your life who offer a positive and optimistic energy and bring out the best in you.

8. **Use a multi-pronged approach.** Don't just lean on one person or activity to manage. It's not fair to burden a single person with the weight of your concerns, nor can they serve all your needs. The more diverse your support system, the better for you and for them. Similarly, each (healthy) activity you pursue will help you differently. Activities to learn more about how to address the problem will strengthen your coping skills, physical activity will maintain your health and energy, and spending quality non-work time with people you love will help you put things in perspective and replenish you emotionally. Consider it like a portfolio: it's important to diversify your resource assets!

See also:

Chapter 1: How To Develop Your Personal Leadership
Chapter 2: Tools That Build Self-Awareness
Chapter 8: How To Build Alliances And Allies Through Strategic Networking

Chapter 33:
How to respond to scapegoating

Ideally, bosses support and praise you in public, and wait for a private meeting to raise criticisms and concerns. Sometimes, however, bosses will say insulting or demeaning things about you in front of others, leaving everyone feeling awkward and you feeling humiliated. When this happens repeatedly publicly and privately, you can become the scapegoat. What do you do in this situation? Read on...

1. **When the scapegoating happens publicly, observe the others in the room to determine if they are also shocked or surprised.** If they are, it will confirm that your feelings and reactions are not misplaced, and these people may become your allies in getting the behavior to stop. If you see scapegoating, most likely other people see it too. Remember you are not alone.

2. **Consider what kind of response may be appropriate now, including perhaps doing nothing.** Resist the urge to snap back at the person in public until you have adequately assessed the situation unless the comment is truly egregious. If it is egregious, sometimes a simple "That's not okay," makes your perspective clear.

3. **If it happens once, consider whether it would make sense to talk with the person in private afterward to let them know that a statement was hurtful and not appropriate.** If possible, engage them in conversation about the statement and determine what is appropriate moving forward. If, however, you're noticing a pattern, it's likely better to understand more about what's going on and address the pattern of behavior instead of approaching your boss about an individual infraction.

4. **Document incidents of insults, even if it's only in your own note log.** Consider emailing notes to yourself so you have a time/date stamp and keep emails that reflect the negative situations. These may be helpful if you need to file a complaint.

5. **If the statement is egregious, sexual, or otherwise highly inappropriate,** consider contacting Human Resources immediately if you have one, even contacting them anonymously, to report the

situation and inquire about appropriate responses. (See Chapter 38 for more on this).

6. **Ask for help.** Identify people who can provide perspective on working with your boss; for example, someone senior to you who works well with your boss or someone who previously worked with your boss. You can say something like, "Sometimes I'm not sure how to interpret what [Boss] is saying, but it doesn't feel good. Can you help me understand your experience with [Boss]?" You can also consider asking a trusted friend or colleague for advice on how to address scapegoating. You can also directly ask a colleague or two to stand up for you in these situations. If you each stand up for each other, your boss will begin to change (and you will have a better case with the organization that it is a widespread problem).

7. **Consider the nature of the work environment.** Some organizations or units within them have a wide tolerance for their leaders to blame junior people for everything that goes wrong. At any time, if you are being targeted for your race/ethnicity, gender/gender expression, disability, age, religion, or being a member of any other "protected class" that is not acceptable.

8. **You may want to consider discussing the situation with a lawyer if you find it unsafe, excessive, persistent, or personalized.** A lawyer represents only you and can help you understand your rights. If you need to find a lawyer, contact a local university law school for an inexpensive or low-cost referral or Google "best employment lawyer" with the name of your town and call to ask for a free consultation.

9. **If this is a persistent pattern that people treat you poorly, you may want to consider obtaining a coach or therapist who can help you through this challenge.**

See also:

Chapter 34.
How to address treatment that appears to be unfair or inequitable

It can come to you like a punch in the gut: you find out a colleague doing the same work has been getting paid more than you or getting plum assignments that you weren't even invited to consider. Sometimes a person more junior to you is hired at a higher rate--to be your boss! Or you are asked to move offices – three times! – for reasons that are still unclear to you and unlike others who were not asked to make the same compromises. While you're steaming about unfairness, inequitable behavior, or behavior that appears to be without purpose or cause, here are some practical suggestions.

1. **Take a deep breath and don't say anything you'll regret later.** Better to figure out what is happening first and provide a reasoned response. Losing your cool only makes you look bad. This is also a demonstration of how developing strong emotional intelligence can help you better evaluate a difficult situation and take greater control of your options before responding.

2. **Recognize that you may not have all the facts.** Something may be seen as unfair because you don't have visibility into the broader context. First seek to understand the context and gather more data before jumping to any conclusions or taking any extreme measures. For example, there are times when there is a lot of movement happening behind the scenes to create positive change that at first may seem quite unfair. Ask a lot of questions to learn more.

3. **See if there are patterns you can identify.** Are the people getting preferential treatment all older, the boss's friends, something else? Who else is this happening to? Try to also sleuth out a counterfactual: what else could explain this situation?

4. **Consider talking with your boss about the perceived inequality.** Keep the focus on the perception and ask politely for an explanation. For example, you could say, "I noticed the last three business trips went to José. Can you help me understand how you make decisions on who gets to go on trips? I'm interested in traveling as well."

5. **If you want to push the issue even further, you can ask the question in a group meeting.** This strategy has risks, can irritate your boss, and may make it less likely you will get what you want. If you decide to address it in a meeting, have pre-conversations with others who will be there and ensure you have allies who will speak up about the issue so that you are not alone in voicing your concern.

6. **If there is a salary issue or something that may not be in your boss's direct control, consider going to Human Resources to ask the question.** Present yourself as curious, not livid. For example, "I happened to find out that there are some significant discrepancies in salary among us managers. Could you help me understand how salaries are determined, and why they are so different when we are doing the same job?" Do not let the other person take the conversation into how you found this information. If they ask about that, say, "Could you confirm whether the discrepancies I'm presenting to you are real? That's more important than how the information came to me." Ideally, they will offer to review salaries and conduct an equity adjustment.

7. **You may want to contact a lawyer if you are not getting information from Human Resources or your boss.** Remember, the company's Human Resources and legal counsel are not primarily employee advocates, but they can assist you in many situations, especially if your interests align with those of the organization. A lawyer can help you understand your options and let you know the likelihood that you will receive the outcome you desire. If you need to find a lawyer, contact a local university law school for an inexpensive or low-cost referral or Google "best employment lawyer" with the name of your town and call to ask for a free consultation. Remember to consider this a last resort after you have tried other lower-level options to get the information you need, get the situation addressed, and seek internal resources. See Chapter 38 on how to best work with Human Resources and legal counsel for more details about when to seek these resources out and how.

8. **Some industries have salary information available.** Contact your trade organization (anonymously if you want) to ask about where to find average salaries for your field. This is a great topic to discuss with a mentor or trusted colleague. Present your observations and

ask how they would proceed. Keep in mind you can win the battle and lose the war--consider the longer-term consequences and whether those are worth it.

9. **Sometimes things aren't fair.** It's wrong and awful and you can't fix it. If this is one of those situations, try to find a way to cope--whether it's leaving the job, moving to another work team, continuing to work toward equity, or accepting things as they are. See Section 2C of this book to help you decide when it's time to move on.

10. **Adjust your expectations about the kind of relationship you can have with your boss, and the kind of guidance they can give you.** Take steps to increase fairness but know you might not have the kind of mentoring relationship you would like.

11. **Remember the importance of equity and ensure you are being fair to others as you advance at work and have more power or employees.** Stand up for staff who are climbing the ladder after you. Work with and get engaged in diversity, equity, and inclusion efforts if they are available at your company. These groups will provide you with the resources and support to help you and others with issues of fairness.

See also:

Chapter 2: Tools That Build Self-Awareness
Chapter 38: How To Best Work With Human Resources And Legal Counsel
Chapter 42: How To Assess Your Options, Make A Decision, And Stick To It

Chapter 35.
How to minimize further harm to yourself

In the most egregious situations in which you are being targeted as a leader by those who seek to remove your power, influence, and status without cause, you might need to resort to more extreme measures of self-protection to keep being effective. Make sure you have tried all the previous recommendations in this book before resorting to these. Some of these may sound alarming, but they are based on real-life experiences and what works to protect yourself from undue harm.

1. **Close ranks.** Consider carefully who can be trusted. Be thoughtful about and limit what you share with whom.
2. **Assume the "Public Persona".** Assume you are always being watched and targeted. Communicate in private and public as if any of it could be shared with the media or others in the organization with whom you did not intend to have the information. Ask yourself in each communication: "Would I say this in front of the news?" "Would I share this on social media?" and "Would I be mortified if this information was released publicly?"
3. **Remove access to information and people.** If you have any concern that a specific person is trying to sabotage your success, block their access to you as much as possible. Remove toxic people from any roles that will create more contagion, especially leadership roles. If these are supervisees, reassign them to other roles to separate them from roles involving access to productive people, sensitive information, and decision-making.
4. **Secure top cover.** In military lingo, to "cover" someone or a team is to protect them from enemy fire, for example, covering soldiers on the ground with air artillery support. Similarly, securing "top cover" within an organization is protecting yourself and your team from incoming "fire" (i.e., awful behavior) from people aiming to destroy your successes. Do this by keeping your superiors and stakeholders close and informed of your work and decisions. Stakeholders include your supervisors as well as those who supervise them and as high up on the reporting chain as you can go. The more you can

communicate your efforts to your key stakeholders, the less likely it is that someone else will be effective at attempts to damage your reputation or credibility. Keep in mind this will require some thoughtful evaluation and calculation of how much you can trust those you inform.

5. **Communicate often with your team about your process to address stressful situations.** If you are actively trying to address harmful behaviors in the organization, make sure to keep your team updated about your efforts as well. Do not badmouth, gossip, or share any details that should remain private (especially anything undergoing a Human Resources review or legal investigation). Focus on just sharing the process you are taking to address the situation rather than the specifics of the content.

6. **Seek consultation and supervision often.** Increase your engagement in consultation and supervision to get as much feedback as you can. Each move you make can have significant ripple effects, so talking through each step and contingencies will help you plan while also protecting you from the greater risk of acting in isolation. Remember to choose wisely what to share and with whom.

7. **Demonstrate proactive crisis management even when it's a reactive situation.** Continue to use as many of the proactive strategies mentioned in Section 1 of this book as you can. It will demonstrate your ability to remain cool under pressure and help the rest of the team feel confident in your ability to lead in stressful situations.

8. **Form power coalitions.** In addition to securing top cover (see #4), seek out trusted stakeholders who are in positions of power. Share with them, without gossiping or badmouthing, the problems you have experienced or witnessed and what you have done to try to address them so far. Seek their advice and help in addressing it. As a coalition of people who have successfully navigated the organizational environment forms – loosely or more formally -- they will likely have great advice and may also be able to protect you from attempts to "take you down."

See also:

Chapter 8: How To Build Alliances And Allies Through Strategic

Networking

Chapter 36.
How to minimize further harm to others

Whether you are the direct target of poor behavior, or someone else is, you have a role to play in protecting others from further harm.

1. **Consider the potential traumatic impact on staff and offer them help or seek help on their behalf.** An individual or team that has endured ongoing harmful behaviors may have experienced emotional and psychological abuse. Even after the source of the problem has been removed, there will be lingering and sometimes long-lasting effects. Some employees will not be affected, while others will be strongly affected. Partner with an internal or external expert in organizational trauma to identify ways to support the staff in managing the impact of the situation, learning healthy ways to cope, and becoming a resilient team.

2. **Protect your well-functioning teams from the negative impact of other harmful teams.** Within an organization, you can find that some teams function incredibly well in the face of an otherwise dysfunctional division or line of business. How? If you are a team leader, you can have a large influence on how well protected your team is from others. Consider how you can serve as their buffer. For example, you can manage stressful interpersonal problems that occur outside the team, without venting to your team about it so they can keep focusing on remaining productive on their own tasks.

3. **Watch for a contagion effect.** Address staff gossip, incivility, and disrespect, directly. Remind them that these behaviors are not aligned with company values. This is one case when it may be helpful to address a problem behavior publicly with the whole team, not just privately with individuals.

4. **Focus on reinforcing positive, supportive engagement.** Create a "tipping point" of positive behaviors that support organizational goals and mission over individual idiosyncratic personal needs that may not be aligned – all may not be on board, but you just need a majority.

5. **Check in, listen to, and validate serious concerns.** Ask individuals and teams how they are doing. Listen carefully for signs that someone is the target of harmful behaviors. Demonstrate compassion. Validate concerns instead of dismissing them. Listen for how you can find a way to help.

6. **Use your power to protect those with less power.** You may not necessarily be at the top of the organization or have limitless power, but everyone has the power to do something. Identify what that power is. What and how much can you get away with in the pursuit of helping others? For some, it might just be the power of listening and supporting – serving as a sounding board. For others, it might be to intervene by asking for clarification when you witness harmful behaviors. Engage at the highest level you can to support those with less power than you.

7. **Intentionally and explicitly state positive messages of support in the face of negative harmful messages you witness.** If you hear another leader or person in a position of power cutting down or insulting someone you know, in addition to potentially addressing that behavior, minimize the potential harm done by offering positive messages or checking in and showing empathy. For example, if you witness someone saying, "Are you kidding me with that presentation? You will never be a leader!" you can later reach out to the target of that harmful comment and say "I heard what Jeremy said to you and I am so sorry you experienced that kind of comment. It wasn't very helpful feedback. I have not experienced you lacking any leadership skills, myself, by the way. Does he talk that way to you often? Do you want to talk about it?"

8. **Remove harmful individuals from access to the team.** If you are in a leadership position in which you can directly remove (or request to directly remove) an individual from the team to minimize harm to others, do so as quickly as possible. Removing the harmful individual addresses both the contagion effect and protecting your team from further harm. This can be done through various mechanisms, including reassigning jobs and roles or taking a more serious Human Resources disciplinary action.

See also:

Chapter 37.
How to intervene on behalf of others

Intervening on behalf of others is just as important as addressing harmful behaviors when they are directed at you. It helps you create the kind of safe environment you want to see for yourself while helping others who are facing these problems directly, and ensures you are not complicit in supporting harmful behaviors to go unaddressed.

1. **Evaluate your contribution.** If you frequently find yourself in the middle of gossip, taunting, or aggressive comments, evaluate whether you are enabling the behavior. For example, if you do not express concern about gossip that is shared with you, or you find yourself laughing at hurtful comments, you are inadvertently contributing to and supporting an unhealthy work environment. Ask yourself what might be getting in the way of responding and seek additional support and feedback.

2. **Speak up for those more vulnerable or with less power so that you can model it for people around you.** This also increases the likelihood they may do the same for you or for others one day. When someone with more power or authority speaks up, it also opens the door for others to add to that comment which may yield constructive feedback and discussions that may not otherwise have occurred. For example, you could say, "Ouch! Can we stop for a moment? Jared, I noticed you said a snide comment just now to Mark. I don't think those kinds of comments are very productive. Is there a concern you have that we can discuss productively?"

3. **Seek training in intervening in difficult conversations.** This includes general communication training, as well as specific topics such as responding to sexual harassment, microaggression, and bullying. Some of the names for these types of trainings include bystander training, restorative justice, and "crucial conversations". The best types of training helps you learn and practice the skills so that you are better prepared in the moment they occur. If you have the opportunity to attend the training together with your coworkers, you

can also refer back to that training in your intervention ("Remember that training we had?")

4. **Try to ask clarifying questions first.** Before making any assumptions or interpretations, seek a way to find out more about the context or reason for someone's behavior. For example: "What did you mean when you said...?"

5. **Use facts, objective observations, and your reaction to describe your concerns.** When you observe concerning behavior, especially when it is not directed toward you, pause and consider what data you have to support your concerns. Then draw attention to the behavior in a nonjudgmental way by simply stating the data you have and how you may have reacted to seeing it, such as, "I saw the door open and you two looked angry. Are you okay?" If you have a closer collegial relationship, you can also use humor: "Boy, I thought there was going to be a boxing match – should I have gotten tickets?!"

6. **Label the behavior, not the person.** When you label a harmful behavior for what it is, with an explanation of how you came to that conclusion, it helps the perpetrator of the behavior understand how their actions are being perceived without feeling unduly attacked for their character. This also helps those who are observing the behavior, and those who are a direct target of the behavior, make sense of the problem they are witnessing. Remember to focus on the facts and not over-interpret. Here's one way to say it: "John, when you shared that personal communication from Gary with the rest of the team, and then questioned his expertise, I really felt like you were trying to undermine him. I don't know whether that was your intention but that's how it came across. Can we talk about what that was about?"

7. **Name patterns of behavior.** This is a powerful method for surfacing ongoing harmful behavior that must stop due to their persistent nature. Behavior that is allowed to persist often gets worse, spreads to others who assume it's okay (contagion effect), and ultimately creates a larger systemic problem that is harder to address. For example, you could say, "Sue, I've noticed that for the past three meetings, you have taken subtle digs at Laura. Last Monday you said to her 'Hope you are prepared this time.' Yesterday, you visibly rolled your eyes and sighed heavily when she shared her updates

with the team. I'm not sure where that is coming from, but the message you are sending is that you are trying to sabotage her success by publicly questioning her competency. Is that your goal?" Notice how many specific behaviors are identified, without judgment, in this comment.

8. **Focus your attention and support on the target of the behavior.** Often the people on the receiving end of harmful behavior are experiencing isolation and feeling singled out or excluded. With no intervention, witnesses may distance themselves from the target to avoid ending up on the receiving end. This sends the wrong message of solidarity and support for the perpetrator. Thus, a quick and powerful intervention is to move toward publicly supporting the person being harmed. In fact, if the harmful behavior feels dangerous or unsafe, the best intervention in the moment is to avoid escalating it and instead support the victim by removing them from the situation, checking on and supporting them, and then deciding a course of action that is safer than directly intervening.

See also:

Chapter 20: How To Ask For (Useful) Feedback
Chapter 25: How To Evaluate The Problem To Choose The Right Solution
Chapter 29: How To Respond To Colleague Gossip And Bad Mouthing

Chapter 38.
How to best work with Human Resources and legal counsel

Sometimes you need to speak to professionals about what's happening at work. Most larger organizations have a Human Resources Office and possibly also legal offices (or general counsel) to ensure the organization is acting lawfully. Seeking Human Resources or legal counsel to address a problematic situation can be an extreme step and best used in situations identified in Chapter 24 (e.g., racism, sexism, harassment, bullying, and other employment discrimination violations).

1. **Seek clarification about Human Resources practices, organizational policies, and local, state, and federal laws.** Consider HR like an internal coach who can offer many resources and advice about how to handle a difficult employee situation. Most of the time, they will offer support, guidance, explanations of policies that may apply, and options (including pros and cons) you can take. They can also approach the situation from multiple legal and policy perspectives. If they feel the behaviors you describe are indeed inappropriate, harmful, and against policy or law, they will let you know your rights and options for that as well. Knowing what the rules are and what your options are can help you learn how to manage difficult situations. It is also helpful to know what is required to document your attempts to resolve the issue more directly (e.g., increasing escalation of interventions, mediation). If you choose to seek guidance from your organization's HR or legal offices, make sure to first ask about any limits to your confidentiality.

2. **Document, document, document.** Document all efforts you have made to reach a resolution or directly address the problem. If you are worried about losing your job or access to your work documents because of the decisions you plan to make, make sure to maintain these documents in your own personal home computer or files. Note that if investigations occur or lawyers get involved, your

documents may be requested for evidence or even subpoenaed. That means that regardless of whether you keep those documents at home or at work, you want to document only the facts, avoid including your judgments of people, and avoid making assumptions of intention. Example of problematic documentation: "Steven was a complete jerk today. His narcissism was toxic. At one meeting, he made me look like a fool and embarrassed me in front of everyone. It's clear he wants me out of my position." Example of strong documentation: "Documented March 20, 2019 at 2:30pm. At the monthly Strong Science meeting when I presented my project, Steven interrupted me three times to talk about his project, and made disparaging comments, such as 'You know, when I was doing a similar project, I found the opposite to be true, but that was a more sophisticated analysis – it's probably why you weren't successful.' He also interrupted Mary, Jean, and Jessica with similar comments. This is the third time I have noticed this behavior across multiple contexts. I have not seen him do this with supervisors or with a few peers he is close to, who all happen to be male."

3. **Be careful what you put in emails or other written material.** Especially if you work for the government or other public non-profit institution, all emails and written materials generated on the job are considered to be public record. That might even include your own private email if you use it for job-related activities. Find out the laws around this. Either way, keep in mind that your communications may be shared with others who may misuse or misinterpret the information. Respond to emails and write material as if they will be published in the media or read by a reporter.

4. **Seek allies.** Facing people who may be actively trying to take power away from you and/or sabotage your success is a stressful, exhausting, and sometimes scary process. Connect with people at work, in your family, or other circles who you trust and can serve as critical emotional support during this time. As with documentation, keep in mind that depending on the actions you take and the severity of the problem, these people may also be requested for evidence or even subpoenaed. Therefore, while venting might feel helpful as a short-term means of managing the

emotional impact of the situation, seeking advice and taking a problem-solving approach will be an important part of managing this situation for multiple reasons, including: (a) demonstrating your attempts at resolving the problem, (b) being proactive in taking control of the situation for yourself, and (c) leaning on your friends, colleagues, and family for guidance, not just a receptacle for complaints. Also, be careful who you choose as an ally. Make sure it is someone who has a long track record demonstrating they have maintained your trust as well as the trust of others. If they sometimes gossip judgmentally about other people, you can be sure they will do the same about you.

5. **Consider seeking additional professional support.** Given the emotional and mental toll that managing harmful behavior can take (and even greater if you are pursuing any HR or legal action), having a professional coach or therapist can help you take time to reflect and work through it. Review the first section of this book for the differences between the two professions and how they can help. As with documentation and seeking allies, keep in mind that depending on the actions you take and the severity of the problem, these people may also be requested for evidence or even subpoenaed. A good professional coach or therapist is well-versed in these issues of confidentiality and access to records and will inform you of your rights and options.

6. **Consider whether to pursue a formal legal or HR action.** Pursuing a formal HR complaint or legal action should be considered a last resort after all else has failed as they require an incredible burden of time (some can take years to resolve), emotional and mental energy, and sometimes money. Additionally, organizations' legal support is focused on protecting the organization, not you. Thus, you need to seek external legal support if you feel you need to protect your job, are seeking compensation for damage, or have seeking other legal outcomes. Given the personal and professional burdens, these HR and legal actions should only be pursued in the most egregious situations that have caused significant long-lasting psychological, financial, and professional damage that may be worth the years of battle to recover. Taking the time to consider the pros and cons of pursuing these options, with guidance from your allies, is critical

given the investment required. See also Section 2C where we talk about when to consider moving on as an alternative option.

7. **Keep a copy of any performance appraisals at home.** If you pursue HR or legal actions, be prepared to potentially have your own professional abilities questioned. If you have been provided with feedback on your past stellar performance, for example, having it readily available will help you defend against inaccurate accusations.

8. **Manage your emotional energy.** Seeking HR or legal action can be emotionally draining. It takes time and may create increased feelings of frustration, impatience, or hopelessness while you gather information and await various parts of the process. Consider it like a marathon: take a steady pace, practice mindfulness, and focus on what you are achieving in the present moment. See also seeking allies and professional support above.

See also:

Chapter 2: Tools That Build Self-Awareness
Chapter 8: How To Build Alliances And Allies Through Strategic Networking
Chapter 42: How To Assess Your Options, Make A Decision, And Stick To It

C: Knowing When to Move On

Chapter 39.
If you are about to get fired

Everyone in your workplace is on edge with nervous looks, talks of budget cuts, and downsizing. Or your boss puts you on a performance improvement plan and lets you know you need to shape up. Either way, if you think you are about to get terminated, here are some things you can do to make a tough situation a little easier.

1. **Update your resume and potential references.** Regardless of how things end up, updating your resume will remind you of your value and experiences, and will make you more prepared if you end up needing to look for work. Don't forget to consider your transferable skills. There may be many opportunities out there to stretch your current experiences into new avenues.

2. **Look at your personal financial situation** and implement cost savings if you can or if you need to, just in case.

3. **If you might get terminated due to performance,** make sure you understand the company's rules about managing performance. Usually, you'll be given a chance to improve. If you want to stay at the company, let them know you want to improve and ask for the help you need.

4. **Keep up with networking.** If layoffs are looming over everyone, it's a good opportunity to meet with colleagues within your organization as well as outside of it to keep your network active. Let people outside your organization know if you're starting to look for other options, but there's no need to share if you're feeling desperate.

5. **Breathe.** This too shall pass. Whatever happens, you are resilient, resourceful, and you have options. No need to panic.

6. **Remember it's almost always better to know the truth** than to worry about what might happen next.

7. **You may want to attend to your personal information.** If you have personal information on your work phone or laptop or computer, go ahead and delete it. Take home any personal files you may have

been storing at work. Backup your contacts or any other information you can remove in case you get terminated.

8. **Don't burn bridges.** Even if you don't agree with the circumstances of how your boss or company handles the termination, be diplomatic.

9. **Be careful sending emails from work.** Your employer has the right to review your work email or may even allow a successor access to your work email so they can keep up with customers or meetings.

10. **Consider talking with your boss about the current situation at your organization.** You may want to ask directly whether you are likely to be terminated (such as if there are rumors of upcoming layoffs). Be aware your boss may not be able to answer you directly.

11. **Consider what your employer might offer if you are terminated,** including health insurance past your termination date, severance pay, how your departure is characterized in your personnel file, how your termination will be referred to when references call, outplacement services, vacation hours payout, and eligibility for unemployment.

12. **You may want to consider obtaining a coach** who can help you through a career transition.

See also:

Chapter 2: Tools That Build Self-Awareness
Chapter 8: How To Build Alliances And Allies Through Strategic Networking
Chapter 40: How To Identify And Re-Prioritize Your Goals

Chapter 40.
How to identify and re-prioritize your goals

If you are considering whether it might be time to move on, it's time for a full evaluation of what's important to you, why you are in this job, and what you want to be doing. Let's dive into the hard work of deciding what to do next.

1. **Consider your big goals.** What do you want to do with your life? Is there a way this job (or having another job) can help you pursue those goals, even if it isn't ideal? If you feel like what you're working toward at your job isn't important or worthwhile, it's okay to move on to a position where you feel like you're making a positive difference.

2. **Consider your values.** If you're working in a field or a role that is no longer compatible with your values, it might be time to move on. When it emerged that a company that I (JW) was working for was doing some shady business, it clarified to me that I needed to find another opportunity. Similarly, if it seems like your boss or many of your colleagues do not share your values, that is important to know, and it suggests it might be time to move on.

3. **Have you learned almost all you can in this job?** Although there's always more to learn, if you're reaching your point of diminishing returns (where you're not continuing to learn new stuff), it might be time to look for something else that will challenge you more.

4. **Remember, you are not under any obligation to try everything you can to make a difficult situation work.** You can leave because you're unhappy, or bored, or for no reason at all. Really. You'll want to think through your decisions and next steps and what you want, but it's perfectly fine to leave. That said, some people feel like they are obligated to try everything possible to prove to themselves that they really tried to make the situation work. You may want to set a target deadline for deciding (for example, 6 months) and gather the data needed to make that decision. Make a checklist of the criteria you feel you need to make your decision and set a path to gather the information needed within that timeline.

5. **How is your health?** Many clients stated they knew it was time to move on only when their health took a nosedive: when they developed an auto-immune disorder, became depressed, started having panic attacks or insomnia, or started having physical symptoms like stomachaches and headaches. It doesn't have to get this bad.

6. **How are your Sunday nights?** For those of you who work Monday through Friday, pay attention to what your Sunday nights feel like. Many people report feeling dread on Sunday night when they know it's time to move on. Identify what you're feeling and if that's how you want to feel. If your dread starts earlier in the day or is very problematic, that's really important information to have.

7. **How are your relationships?** Are your friendships suffering? Is this affecting your partner, children, or other family members or your connection to them? Many clients tell us they knew it was time to go when their relationships started suffering consistently due to their work situation.

8. **Some situations make it easy to walk:** harassment, unethical behavior, narcissistic boss. Those are good signs it's time to get out. You don't have to be a martyr and stick it out, even if it's for a good cause like protecting others. It's okay to take care of your needs too.

9. **If you're feeling anxious just thinking about these goals, that is okay.** Breathe and recognize you're just reassessing. What you discover about yourself in this situation does not compel you to take any immediate action. Try to understand what about this process is making you anxious. Spend some time writing or doodling to help you think through this section in a way that helps you acknowledge your feelings and see what's in front of you.

See also:

Chapter 1: How To Develop Your Personal Leadership
Chapter 32: How To Manage The Personal Toll Of Unhealthy Workplace Behaviors
Chapter 42: How To Assess Your Options, Make A Decision, And Stick To It

Chapter 41.
How to know when it's time to move on

Choosing to move on from a job or career in the face of difficult politics – or for any other reason – is NOT failure. It is a continued step in your long life. Similarly, assessing a difficult situation and choosing to stay is also NOT failure. And the best part is that either choosing to leave or to stay are decisions you can reassess. If you find that you have gone through all these steps, it may be a message that it's time to leave.

1. **Leaving has multiple steps.** Deciding to leave or stay is a process, not a one-time event! Don't expect to work through all of this in an hour. Here are the steps to leaving:
   a. *Increasing awareness* that the current situation is no longer meeting your needs.
   b. *Working through the messy middle.* This is the transition between where you are now and where you might be headed, when you are not sure what you might do next. It might feel like forever. You might feel lost at sea without a compass. Use this time to keep gathering data and look for signs about what you need to make a next-step decision.
   c. *Experiencing hope* that leaving can make things better related to your ability to meet your goals, be healthy, feel comfortable at work, feel like you're making a difference, or anything else that you want to be better.
   d. *Gaining confidence* that leaving will lead to something better. Many people worry they'll just find the same problems wherever they go. Everywhere has problems; it's a matter of what problems bother you and what don't. A partner snoring is a dealbreaker for some light sleepers and not a problem at all for deep sleepers.
   e. *Making the decision* to investigate leaving (organization or position).
   f. *Preparing for departure*, including applying and interviewing for new positions, preparing your team (both before and after you announce you're leaving), managing the announcement, and

taking care of all other issues (e.g., family, moving, packing, etc.)

    g.   *Leaving.* Turning in your badge, or walking out the door with your plant, or just walking out is its own moment.

    h.   *Integrating your journey.* Over time, we soften the challenges and smooth the edges. This allows us to have more perspective on what our journey has been and what we want to do next.

2. **If you haven't already, assess your situation** as indicated in *Chapter 40: How to identify and re-prioritize your goals.* Having your goals, feelings, values, and health considerations in front of you, so it's on paper and not swirling around in your head (!) can be very helpful. Feel free to add to it as items come up.

3. **Go deeper into your situation and write out what you like and don't like about your job.** This could be framed in positive and negative aspects of your job or in a different way. Some of these aspects may be related to each other because they differ by degrees; for example, it may be that you enjoy the competitive environment that pushes you to be more innovative, and at the same time you don't like dealing with some of the overly competitive people. Write it all out. It may be helpful to also rate, on a scale of 1 to 10, how important each positive and negative aspect of your job is to your decision-making to further clarify your priorities and next steps.

4. **If you're thinking you want to leave, take this a step further, and make a 2 x 2 table: Pros vs. cons of staying vs. going.** Many times, this step makes it clear what you want to do. Sometimes it's more of a gut or emotional feeling. Write that out too.

5. **Consider if you need to leave your department, company, or field.** Leaving doesn't have to mean leaving the entire company. There may be wonderful parts of your company that are insulated from whatever challenges are plaguing you now. You can decide if you want to consider other within-company options, a different company in the same field, or a different field altogether!

6. **It's useful to get opinions from trusted mentors, family, or friends about whether you should leave.** Recognize that everyone has their own anxieties and strengths about moving on: some people get very nervous when thinking about leaving and try to pass that on to you by telling you awful stories of how you won't make it, or you're

safer to stay here, or that "people will think" poorly of you. Use what is useful for you, and don't take on their anxieties. At this point, only talk with people you completely trust to keep information confidential. The best people to talk with are those you have seen successfully navigate a complicated transition and those who know you and your values and skills well.

7. **Continue writing out and considering what you might need to think about related to leaving.** You can add to some of the above lists by indicating financial considerations, worries (that you follow up on by doing your own research or talking it out), lists of possible other employers, mentors who could write letters of recommendation or open doors for you … the list of possibilities is endless! Whatever is in your head at this point, keep getting it out of your head and onto paper so your brain can continue to process it.

8. **Allow time for reflection.** At least once a week, take some time to review what you've learned and ensure you're on the right track. Identify what you really enjoy about your job and what you don't care for. Ideally, you want a job that has lots of what you enjoy and a minimal amount of what you don't care for. How can you make that happen?

9. **Plan your future mindfully and take advantage of unexpected opportunities to learn and grow.** Learn and grow from everything! Chance favors the prepared mind.

See also:

Chapter 25: How To Evaluate The Problem And Choose The Right Solution
Chapter 40: How To Identify And Re-Prioritize Your Goals
Chapter 42: How To Assess Your Options, Make A Decision, And Stick To It

Chapter 42
How to assess your options, make a decision, and stick to it

Leaving a job is often challenging, and it's even more complicated when you have staff you'll leave behind. Once you've decided to make the leap, here are some ideas for how you can make the transition as smoothly as possible.

1. **Talk with people who have made daring career moves.** Ask them how they knew it was time to make a leap, how they prepared, what they regret, and how it worked out. Ask for advice if it's appropriate.

2. **Prepare what you will say when people find out about your departure.** Come up with a statement that is authentic to who you are and that doesn't put down your employer, boss, or other staff at the organization where you were. If you don't want to share where you're going next, you don't have to, but know people will ask and be curious. Prepare answers to questions and comments you will likely hear, such as, "Take me with you!" or "I knew you weren't happy here," or "The [boss] really was a jerk, weren't they?" Be respectful and don't speak ill of anyone on your way out. It may seem like it will be satisfying, but it's not in your interest in the long run. Remember not to burn bridges.

3. **Consider what projects you may need to wrap up and anything you want to ensure is finished before you go.** Work on these to ensure they end how you want them to. Put files as appropriate on the shared drives if available and clean up your email folders. Leave clear instructions (or train others) for anything that will need some transitional maintenance between you and your successor.

4. **Continue preparing your staff for greater leadership roles by having them step into meetings, learn about what you're doing, and ask questions so they learn.** You can do this whether you've told them you're leaving or not.

5. **Prepare how you will tell people you're leaving.** I prepare a list of people I will tell in person (including my staff), people I will call on the phone, and people I will email. Remember, once you tell the first

person, news will start getting out. I (JW) schedule all these meetings on the same day to have the leaving conversations, then make phone calls, and send the email at the end of the day. It will be an exhausting day, so make sure to plan something nice for yourself after work.

6. **If you've had a particularly awful work experience or if you struggle with transitions,** consider visiting a therapist or professional coach to work through challenges and help you let it go.

7. **Prep your friends/family outside of work to provide support to you during this time.** Ask for what you need.

8. **Consider little rituals that might help you close out the last chapter,** such as updating your resume or LinkedIn, getting new business cards or a uniform for the new job, and celebrating with your friends.

9. **Remember there's a substantial emotional component to leaving a job.** Give yourself time to process changing your commute, losing some friends, leaving an employer you've known. Even if you're happy to move on, give yourself space for whatever feelings may arise.

10. **Reflect on your work experience.** What did you do well, what could you do better, what did you learn? Then let it go and step forward into the rest of your life.

11. **Keep in touch with those you value.** Saying goodbye to a company doesn't always mean goodbye to everything. There may be people you really loved working with. Stay in touch. You never know how those relationships might continue to grow and lead to other future opportunities. For example, a peer or mentor you highly value and respect may some day take a new leadership role that changes the company and gets you excited to work for or with them under those different circumstances.

See also:

FINAL THOUGHTS

A few final words as you go forth and conquer that political terrain.

Stand strong. You are a force for good. You are here to lead people to higher ground and to get stuff done. Find your strength, find your center, and kick some ass!

Recognize your limits. You can't save everyone, and you can't fix everything.

Set priorities. Consider what is important to your organization, boss, constituents, and to you. Don't forget what's important to you, whether that's reflective of your values or of what you want to have accomplished when it's time to move on.

Surround yourself with a support team. Remember there are allies, champions, mentors, coaches, therapists, friends, and family members who can all serve to keep you going. You don't have to be alone in managing any challenge – you just need to be savvy about it.

Own your power. You can make a big impact. You just need to own your power and not shy away from it.

FOR FURTHER READING

Power and Politics

1. Brancu, Mira. (2019, June 04). Five Recommendations for Engaging in Honest Politics at Work. Retrieved February 23, 2021, from https://www.psychologytoday.com/us/blog/new-look-womens-leadership/201906/five-recommendations-engaging-in-honest-politics-work

2. Dominguez, Linda R. (2003). *How to Shine at Work*. McGraw-Hill, New York.

3. Kusy, Mitchell and Elizabeth Holloway. (2009). *Toxic Workplace: Managing Toxic Personalities and Their Systems of Power*. Jossey-Bass, San Francisco.

4. McClelland, David C. and David H. Burnham. (2003, January). *Power Is the Great Motivator*. Harvard Business Review, Boston, MA. Retrieved February 23, 2021 from https://hbr.org/2003/01/power-is-the-great-motivator

5. Pfeffer, Jeffrey. (2010). *Power: Why Some People Have It and Others Don't*. Harper Business, New York.

Developing Your Own Leadership Style

1. Brandon, Rick and Marty Seldman. (2004). *Survival of the Savvy: High Integrity Political Tactics for Career and Company Success*. Free Press, New York.

2. Flynn, Jill, Kathryn Heath, and Mary Davis Holt. (2011). *Breaking Your Own Rules: How to Change the Patterns of Thinking that Block Women's Paths to Power*. Jossey-Bass, San Francisco.

3. Harvard Business Review. (2019). *HBR Guide for Women at Work*. Harvard Business Review, Boston.

4. Heath, Kathryn, Jill Flynn, Mary Davis Holt, and Diana Faison. (2017). The *Influence Effect: A New Path to Power for Women Leaders*. Berrett-Koehler Publishers, San Francisco.

5. Kilburg, Richard R. (2012). *Virtuous Leaders: Strategy, Character, and Influence in the 21st Century*. American Psychological Association, Washington, DC.

6. Wisdom, Jennifer P. (2020). *Millennials' Guide to Management & Leadership: What No One Ever Told You About How to Excel as a Leader.* Winding Pathway Books, New York.

Communication and Emotional Intelligence
1. Bradberry, Travis, and Jean Greaves. (2009). *Emotional Intelligence 2.0.* TalentSmart, San Diego, CA
2. Covey, Stephen. (1989). *The Seven Habits of Highly Effective People.* Simon & Schuster, New York.
3. Goleman, Daniel. (2005). *Emotional intelligence: Why It Can Matter More than IQ.* Bantam, New York.
4. Patterson, Kerry, Joseph Grenny, Ron McMillan, and Al Switzler. (2011). *Crucial Conversations: Tools for Talking When Stakes Are High.* McGraw-Hill Education, New York.
5. Rogelberg, Steven G. (2019). *The Surprising Science of Meetings: How You Can Lead Your Team to Peak Performance.* Oxford University Press, New York.
6. Su, Amy Jen, and Muriel Maignan Wilkins. (2013). *Own the room: Discover your signature voice to master your leadership presence.* Harvard Business Review Press, Boston.
7. Eisenberg, Eric M., and Sean Mahar. (2019). *Stop Wasting Words: Leading Through Conscious Communication.* Advantage Media Group. New York.

Negotiation
1. Babcock, Linda, and Sara Laschever. (2008). *Ask for it: How Women Can Use Negotiation to Get What They Really Want.* Bantam, New York.
2. Cohen, Allan R. and David L. Bradford. (2017). *Influence Without Authority.* Wiley, Hoboken, NJ.
3. Fisher, Roger and William Ury. (2012). *Getting to Yes: Negotiating an Agreement Without Giving In.* Random House Business Books, New York.
4. Mnookin, Robert. (2011). *Bargaining with the Devil: When to Negotiate, When to Fight.* Simon & Schuster, New York.
5. Shell, G. Richard. (2006). *Bargaining for Advantage: Negotiation Strategies for Reasonable People.* Penguin Books, New York.

Leading and Managing Teams

1. Edmondson, Amy C. (2014). *Teaming: How Organizations Learn, Innovate, and Compete in the Knowledge Economy.* Jossey-Bass Pfeiffer, San Francisco, CA.
2. Hackman, J. Richard, and Richard J. Hackman. (2002). *Leading teams: Setting the stage for great performances.* Harvard Business Press, Boston.
3. Katzenbach, Jon R. and Douglas K. Smith. (2015). *The Wisdom of Teams: Creating the High-Performance Organization.* Harvard Business Review, Boston.
4. Lencioni, Patrick. (2009). Five Dysfunctions of a Team: A Leadership Fable. Jossey-Bass, San Francisco.
5. Rogelberg, Steven G. (2019). *The Surprising Science of Meetings: How You Can Lead Your Team to Peak Performance.* Oxford University Press, New York.
6. Tuckman, Bruce W., and Mary Ann C. Jensen. (2010). Stages of small-group development revisited. *Group Facilitation: A Research & Applications Journal* (10), 43-48.

Toxic Workplaces and Difficult People

1. Benjamin, Susan. (2007). *Perfect Phrases for Dealing with Difficult People: Hundreds of Ready-to Use Phrases for Handling Conflicts, Confrontations and Challenging Personalities.* McGraw-Hill Education, New York.
2. Bernstein, Albert J. (2000). *Emotional Vampires: Dealing with People Who Drain You Dry.* McGraw-Hill, New York.
3. Bramson, Robert M. (1988). *Coping with Difficult People.: The Proven-Effective Battle Plan That Has Helped Millions Deal with the Troublemakers in Their Lives at Home and at Work.* Dell, New York.
4. Dillon, Karen. (2014). *Harvard Business Review Guide to Office Politics.* Harvard Business Review, Boston.
5. Evenson, Renee. (2014). *Powerful Phrases for Dealing with Difficult People.* Amacom, New York.
6. Frankel, Lois P. (2004). *Nice Girls Don't Get the Corner Office: 101 Unconscious Mistakes Women Make That Sabotage Their Careers.* Business Plus, New York.

7. Kusy, Mitchell and Elizabeth Holloway. (2009). *Toxic Workplace: Managing Toxic Personalities and Their Systems of Power.* Jossey-Bass, San Francisco.

8. Sue Derald Wing, Christina M. Capodilupo, Gina C. Torino, Jennifer M. Bucceri, Aisha M. Holder, Kevin L. Nadal, and Marta Esquilin. (2007). Racial microaggressions in everyday life: implications for clinical practice. *The American Psychologist,* 62(4), 271–86.

9. Sutton, Robert I. (2018). *The Asshole Survival Guide: How to Deal with People Who Treat You Like Dirt.* Mariner Books, Boston.

10. Swindling, Linda Byars. (2013). *Stop Complainers and Energy Drainers: How to Negotiate Work Drama to Get More Done.* Wiley, Hoboken, NJ.

ACKNOWLEDGEMENTS

We wish to thank Lindsay Harris, Dick Kilburg, Tanida Mullen, Gerry Vogel, Greg Muriello, Olivia Nadasan, Lynn Potts, Kristin Powell, Kate Scott, Stefanie Mockler, NaTasha Jordan, and Holly Whitelaw for their exceptional and kind feedback, ideas, and encouragement. A special thank you to Olivia Nadasan, Kate Scott, and Stefanie Mockler for providing early and significant feedback that helped us add more examples of real experiences and include critical sections of interest. We additionally thank Cassandra Blake for exemplary administrative assistance, Diego G. Diaz and Allie Mullin for photography, and Diego G. Diaz for cover design.

Dr. Mira Brancu would also like to thank her husband, Dr. Jeffrey Greene, for enduring many months of her being holed up in her office typing away - and spending an equal number of months listening patiently while she chewed his ear off about this book. His support and insights for how this book could also meet the needs of his own students and early career faculty in academia were invaluable. She would also like to thank her children for their patience while she called out "One more minute!"... for what likely amounted to thousands (maybe millions!) of minutes of writing on nights and weekends. She also sends a special thank you to her parents, Victor and Victoria Brancu (yes, they have matching names!) for the many opportunities they bestowed upon her through one brave action: emigrating to the US in their mid-30's with two very young children (Mira and her brother Ted) to offer them a better life. Learning to navigate a complex new language and culture was her first experience with some of the lessons in this book. Finally, Mira would like to thank her previous supervisor and mentor, Dr. John Fairbank. After previously struggling to successfully navigate politics in a totally different career and setting, John helped her identify strengths she never knew she possessed, as well as uncover and overcome blind spots that could hold her back from succeeding in a new large, complex organization. This gave her the courage and skills to make huge brave leaps in her career and reach levels of leadership success beyond what she ever expected of herself. It also led to her current career path, and the passion to provide other women and those from marginalized groups access to the same information she was fortunate enough to receive. It's all in this book.

ABOUT THE AUTHORS

Mira Brancu, PhD MEd, is a leadership and team development consulting psychologist, executive coach, author, and speaker. As a leader and consultant, Mira has earned a reputation for her ability to teach others how to effectively navigate complex systems; align personal, professional, and organizational priorities to meet goals; capitalize on individual and team strengths to drive excellence; develop strategic thinking and processes; and work effectively with individuals, teams, and organizations. She has worked within large complex systems such as healthcare, government, and academic industries for over 20 years, including Duke University and the Department of Veterans Affairs. Dr. Brancu is also the CEO of Brancu & Associates, a leadership and team development consulting company. She can be reached at *www.brancuassociates.com.*

Jennifer P. Wisdom, PhD MPH ABPP, is an author, consultant, speaker, and principal of Wisdom Consulting. As a consultant, she helps curious, motivated, and mission-driven professionals to achieve their highest potential by identifying goals and then providing them with the roadmap and guidance to get there. Jennifer created the best-selling *Millennials' Guides* series, including *Millennials' Guide to Work, Millennials' Guide to Management & Leadership, Millennials' Guide to Relationships,* and *Millennials' and Generation Z Guide to Voting.* Dr. Wisdom is a licensed clinical psychologist and board-certified organizational psychologist with post graduate training in public health. She has worked with complex health care, government, and educational environments for 25 years, including serving in the U.S. military, working with non-profit service delivery programs, and as faculty in higher education. She is an intrepid adventurer based in New York City and Portland, Oregon. She can be reached at *www.leadwithwisdom.com.*